# Understanding the Media in Young Children's Lives

This book explores the impact of digital media on young children's lives and the role that the media and news industries play in the social construction of childhood. It highlights the pressing issues relating to young children's media use drawing on key research and examines the impact of digital media on their learning, development and socialisation.

The chapters recognise the challenges digital media presents children and families, but also demonstrate how media use and engagement can have a positive impact on children's academic attainment, social capital and opportunities to create and curate online content. Covering key areas of concern such as safety, violence and children's mental health, the authors provide strategies to help children and families reduce the risks that can arise with digital media use and capitalise on the opportunities it can offer.

Including case study examples and opportunities for reflective practice, this is an essential text for students on Childhood and Early Childhood Studies courses and Early Years Foundation Degrees, as well as practitioners wanting to develop their critical understanding of the role of the media in young children's lives.

**Polly Bolshaw** is a Senior Lecturer in Early Years at Canterbury Christ Church University. Previously she worked as an Early Years Professional in a Sure Start Children's Centre. Research interests include the impact of the media on children's lives and research methods for undergraduate students.

**Jo Josephidou** is Programme Lead for Early Childhood at The Open University. Previously she has worked as an Early Years school teacher. Research interests include appropriate pedagogies for young children, babies' and toddlers' engagement with nature and issues around gender in ECEC.

# Understanding the Media in Young Children's Lives

## An Introduction to the Key Debates

Polly Bolshaw
Jo Josephidou

Routledge
Taylor & Francis Group
LONDON AND NEW YORK

Cover image: Getty number: 800944140

First edition published 2023
by Routledge
4 Park Square, Milton Park, Abingdon, Oxon, OX14 4RN

and by Routledge
605 Third Avenue, New York, NY 10158

*Routledge is an imprint of the Taylor & Francis Group, an informa business*



*British Library Cataloguing-in-Publication Data*
A catalogue record for this book is available from the British Library

*Library of Congress Cataloging-in-Publication Data*
A catalog record has been requested for this book

ISBN: 978-0-367-63896-2 (hbk)
ISBN: 978-0-367-63898-6 (pbk)
ISBN: 978-1-003-12120-6 (ebk)

DOI: 10.4324/9781003121206

Typeset in Palatino
by codeMantra

*To George and Emmie*

# Contents

# Illustrations

## Tables



## Figure

CHAPTER

# 1 Introduction

Wherever you are in the world, it is safe to say that digital media use has never been greater. Children have become accustomed to the opportunities that digital media can offer for learning, with many proficient in taking part in classrooms online rather than in their school buildings. Similarly, most are familiar with socialising online, with many having experience of family catch-ups virtually via videocall rather than face-to-face. Tablet ownership amongst children has never been higher, nor has the number of children with social media profiles. Thus, considering children's digital media lives has never been more important. This book recognises the new challenges around digital media use facing children and families as a result of the changing world but also acknowledges the benefits of children's media lives and what approaches may allow children and families to reduce the threats that can arise with digital media use and instead capitalise on the opportunities it can offer.

## What is this book about?

This book will encourage you to question why it is more relevant than ever to consider young children's media lives, both in relation to traditional and digital media. We will explore how media use and engagement can have a positive impact on children's academic attainment, social capital and opportunities to create and curate online content. We will then consider some aspects thought to be negative, such as inappropriate content and children's mental health; the role that the media and in particular the news industry plays in the social construction of childhood; and the media literacy strategies that may minimise the risks of young children engaging in digital media use.

We have found that children's media use is often an emotive topic, as adults talk about how 'in their day' they spent lots of time playing outside, but this time has been eroded away by (a) parents' reluctance to let their children play outside (fuelled by the news media's focus on stranger danger) and (b) children's love of digital technologies. Often our students share anecdotal examples about the children they know and extrapolate to share 'facts' about what 'all children' are doing online, how old they were when they got their first mobile and how they

DOI: 10.4324/9781003121206-1

want to be a vlogger or social media influencer when they grow up. This book encourages students to take these anecdotes as a starting point but think critically about them to explore whether they are supported (or not) by research and theory, and how indeed these perspectives are potentially fuelled by the moral panic that newspapers, in particular, create.

## How to use this book

We have written this book with the intention that you will engage with it in an active way. There are moments where we might ask you to have a think about something before moving on. Sometimes you'll see content presented in tables, figures and bullet points, which are designed to help you to digest the information. And to support you to take in and reflect upon the contents of this book, we have also included some *Time to consider* exercises. Although you might be tempted to skip past them, completing these will enable you to get the most out of this text, help you to consolidate your learning and support you in developing your critical thinking and analysis skills. They take a variety of forms; you may be asked to complete a table, read a journal article, design a poster, or simply spend some time reflecting. Here is the first one, have a go at completing it. Keep your notes somewhere safe so you can add to them each time you get to a new *Time to consider* exercise.

### Time to consider

Take some time to reflect on how children are portrayed in the media that you access. Make some notes on the following questions:

- How do you see children represented on the television shows you watch?
- What about the advertisements you come across? And in the newspapers you read?
- Do you think that they give accurate representations of children's lives and what children are like? If not, why do you think this might be?

## Who is this book for?

This book is for anyone who wants to develop their understanding of the most pressing issues relating to children's media use in early childhood and who wants to critique the role of the media in the lives of young children. You might be working with young children at the moment, or just studying them. You might be thinking about a future career in education, social care or children's health. Whoever you are, it is important that you have an awareness of the impact of media usage on aspects such as children's academic achievements, social lives

**TABLE 1.1** Reflecting on your own media usage

| How much time in the average day do you spend ... |
|---|
| Browsing the internet? |
| Watching television or streaming services? |
| Listening to the radio? |
| Playing video games? |
| Using apps on your phone? |

and health, and begin to critique this usage. But it is also key that you reflect honestly about your own media use. Think about how that might influence your perceptions and views of children's usage. Also consider how it might impact on the information that is communicated to you about children's lives, for instance from stories, images and posts you see shared on social media, news reports you read or in the television programmes you watch. To help you think about your own media usage, have a go at completing Table 1.1.

Once you have completed that, now think about the children that you know. What do you think their media use is like? How does it compare to your media usage when you were a child? And what do you think the implications of children's media use might be? These are the questions we will be thinking about throughout this book.

### Time to consider

Whether you are working with young children, or studying them, or both, it is always useful when you start considering a new topic to think about what you already know about it. Take a piece of paper and make a spider diagram about what you already know in relation to the media and early childhood. You might already know information about what children's media use is like and what the impacts are perceived to be of this media use. You might know from your personal or professional lives how children that you are in contact with are engaging with digital technologies. This information is useful to reflect upon, too.

## What can you expect to read in this book?

The rest of this book is going to continue to develop your knowledge about children and their media use. It is divided up into three parts. In the first part, we are going to explore what some of the positive and negative impacts of children's media use are argued to be. For instance, in Chapter 3 (*Children's media as education, not entertainment*) we will be exploring the extent to which media use can have a positive impact on children's academic attainment. We will look at educational programmes like *Sesame Street* and the role they play in supporting children's learning; for instance we will consider how Mares and Pan (2013) have identified that the programme can provide benefits in children's cognitive outcomes (like literacy and numeracy), understanding the world and social reasoning. We will also consider young children's tablet use and some of the findings of the ongoing TABLET (Toddler Attentional Behaviours and LEarning with Touchscreens) project, which is investigating young children's use of touchscreen technology and the links with their cognitive and social development.

Then in Chapter 4 (*Viewing violence: Just a moral panic?*) we will think about how media usage can have a negative impact on children's development, for instance when children view violent material. We will use the work of Bandura and his social learning theory to consider from a theoretical perspective what might happen when children consume violent content. We will continue considering some of the negative impacts in Chapter 5 (*Media and children's health*) too, when we will explore what the impacts of media use can be on a child's mental and physical health. Some recent reports including by Frith (2017) and the Royal Society of Public Health (2017) identify that social media in particular can have a detrimental impact on children's mental health, such as in increasing feelings of anxiety and depression, facilitating opportunities for cyber-bullying, detracting from sleep, and leading to a fear of missing out (FOMO). Yet social media can potentially have positive effects on children and young people's mental health too, for instance through supporting them to make and maintain relationships, which can be particularly important for those with disabilities or special educational needs (SEN).

As we move on to Chapter 6 (*Children as consumers: The impact of advertising*) we will progress to Part 2 of this book and shift focus to think about how types of media construct childhood and the indirect influences they can have over children's lives. Chapter 6 considers children and advertising. We will look at how children are sometimes portrayed in adverts and as part of this will consider some fascinating research by O'Dell (2008) who has looked at the portrayal of children in charity adverts. In this chapter we will also consider some research by the Advertising Standards Authority (ASA) (2012) about what children and their parents think about different types of adverts and what sometimes concerns them about the television advertisements they come across.

Chapter 7 (*Innocent, invisible or feral: Constructions of children in the media*) then considers the portrayal of children in news media. Lindon (2011) talks about the way that children are depicted in the media and how this swings between two extremes – on the one hand as overly innocent beings, or on the other as unruly thugs and hooligans. We will consider what impact such a portrayal might have on children, and also look at literature from Jones (2014) about the death of Peter Connolly (known in the media as 'Baby P') and the media coverage of other children such as Madeline McCann and Shannon Matthews. Following this, in Chapter 8 (*Helpful theoretical lenses: How theory can help us understand children's engagement with the media*) we will consider some helpful theoretical frameworks for understanding children's engagement with the media. We will start by looking at children's media use through the lens of Bronfenbrenner's ecological systems theory, before considering it in relation to Bourdieu's concepts of habitus, field and forms of capital. After that we will think about how Postman's work has contributed to the debates around children's media engagement.

Finally, the third part of this book considers what strategies we can put in place to minimise the risks and capitalise on the opportunities that children's media use can bring, by thinking about how we can develop children's media literacy skills. In Chapter 9 (*Born digital: Promoting young children's media literacy*) we will explore what media literacy and digital literacy are and why they are important. Then in Chapter 10 (*Children and new digital media: The risks and the benefits*) we will be thinking about what strategies we can put in place to develop media literacy skills, both of children, and of their parents and the teachers and early years practitioners that come into contact with them. For instance, we will think about research from Nominet that has looked at what information parents are sharing about their children via social media, for instance photographs and details about their lives, and what the impact of these digital footprints might be. We will consider apps such as Tapestry that act as online learning journals for children in Early Childhood Education and Care (ECEC) settings, where practitioners upload details, photos and videos of the child's day, as well as the growing use of surveillance cameras in early years settings that allow parents to log on via an app and observe what their children are doing in real time.

Next, in Chapter 11 (*Understanding how research on children's media lives is conducted*) we will be exploring how research on children's media lives is conducted and consider and critique some of the methodological decisions made. We will explore both large- and small-scale studies from the disciplines of education and psychology and encourage you to think about how you could design your own piece of research about children's media lives. Finally, in Chapter 12 (*Bringing it all together*) we will sum up the big ideas the book has raised and bring all of our thinking together.

## Time to consider

One of the questions that this book may raise for you is about whether the potential benefits of children's media usage and engagement outweigh the potential disadvantages of their media usage and engagement. Make a table like Table 1.2 to help you decide whether you think the advantages may be more significant than the drawbacks. As you continue through this book, keep coming back to this table and add to it.

**TABLE 1.2** The benefits and risks of children's media usage and engagement

| Benefits of children's media usage | Disadvantages of children's media usage |
|---|---|
| | |

## Final reflection

We hope that you find this text useful in building your knowledge about children's media lives, both historically and in the twenty-first century, both in the UK and internationally. As we have said, we know students in particular often rely on anecdotal evidence about the children they know when talking and writing about children's media use. This book will introduce you to key pieces of published research and stress the importance of considering these to help you understand more fully the experiences of children you might know. It will also support you in linking those real-life experiences to theoretical lenses that you can view children's experiences through. In this way, you will be in a strong position to critique young children's media lives in an objective way, conscious that the amount of time children are engaging with both traditional and digital media is ever increasing.

## Key points

- To fully understand young children's lives, we need an awareness of the important role that digital media plays in their learning, development and socialisation.
- We need to be conscious of how media sources, in particular television and newspapers, choose to portray and represent children as this consequently impacts on how they are perceived and treated in wider society.
- This book is split up into three sections. The first part explores what some of the positive and negative impacts of children's media use are argued to be. The second considers how types of media construct childhood and the indirect influences they can have over children's lives. The final section reflects on what strategies we can put in place to minimise the risks and capitalise on the opportunities that children's media use can bring.

## References

Advertising Standards Authority (2012) *Public Perceptions of Harm and Offence in UK Advertising*. Available at: www.asa.org.uk/asset/DDB37644-FE4C-448E-9EC6F17E1DD1DF5D/ (accessed 29 August 2021).

Frith, E. (2017) *Social Media and Children's Mental Health: A Review of the Evidence*. Available at: https://epi.org.uk/wp-content/uploads/2017/06/Social-Media_Mental-Health_EPI-Report.pdf (accessed 29 August 2021).

Jones, R. (2014) *The Story of Baby P: Setting the Record Straight*. Bristol: Policy Press.

Lindon, J. (2011) *Too Safe for Their Own Good?* London: NCB.

Mares, M. and Pan, Z. (2013) 'Effects of Sesame Street: A Meta-Analysis of Children's Learning in 15 Countries', *Journal of Applied Developmental Psychology*, 34(3), pp. 140–151.

O'Dell, L. (2008) 'Representations of the "Damaged" Child: "Child Saving" in a British Children's Charity Ad Campaign', *Children & Society*, 22(5), pp. 383–392.

Royal Society for Public Health (2017) *#StatusofMind*. Available at: www.rsph.org.uk/static/uploaded/d125b27c-0b62-41c5-a2c0155a8887cd01.pdf (accessed 29 August 2021).

PART

I

# What are positive and negative impacts of children's media use?

CHAPTER

# 2 Children's media lives

We imagine that shortly before picking up this book, you will have glanced at your mobile, closed down your laptop or switched off the television. Or alternatively, you might not be reading this as a physical book at all, but instead are engaging with this text in a digital format on your e-reader, tablet or phone. Suffice to say, we know that digital media usage is a big, and growing, part of our lives. The same is true for young children – the amount of time young children are spending online and engaging with digital media is increasing. That is why it is important that we think critically about the role that the media is playing in the lives of young children, which is what this first chapter will begin to consider.

## How are we defining children's media usage?

A good place to start in this book is with some definitions of what we mean by the idea of 'media'. We know that some people use the term 'media' interchangeably with 'technology'. We also know that in some instances the word 'media' is preceded by further definers such as 'social', 'digital' or 'traditional'. Our definition of media activities is informed by Ofcom (2016a) who categorised children's media and communications activities for the purpose of conducting a piece of research that explored children's and adults' media usage. It was called 'The Digital Day' (Ofcom, 2016a).

Ofcom divide media and communications usage into 28 activities. These activities are then categorised into five themes: watching, listening, communicating, playing, and reading/browsing/using. It is useful to break down the different types of media usage in this way; it can be easy to think of 'children engaging with media' as a whole, but as you can see in Table 2.1 there are many differences in what children may be doing, the skills they may be learning, and the competences they may need to have, dependent on the type of media activity they are undertaking. It is also important to remember two other points when thinking about the different types of media activities. Some, like watching and listening, are perhaps more likely to be done as a group activity, whilst others like gaming and reading are more of a solo pastime.

DOI: 10.4324/9781003121206-3

**TABLE 2.1** Ofcom's (2016a) media activities and definitions

| Category | Activity |
|---|---|
| **Watching** | TV (live – at the time it is broadcast, including using the red button) |
| | Recorded TV (programmes or films stored on your personal/digital recorder box using e.g. TiVo, Sky+ or Freeview+) |
| | On-demand/catch-up TV or films (free), e.g. BBC iPlayer, All 4, Sky or Virgin on demand |
| | Downloaded or streamed digital TV or films (paid-for), e.g. Amazon Instant Video, Netflix, iTunes, Blinkbox, Sky Store, Disney Life |
| | TV or films on DVD, Blu-ray, VHS video |
| | Short online video clips on e.g. YouTube, News sites (including those through social networking sites) |
| **Listening** | Radio (at the time of broadcast) |
| | On-demand/'Listen again' radio programmes or podcasts |
| | Personal digital music or audio collection (e.g. on an iPod, smartphone, computer, etc.) |
| | Streamed online music (e.g. Spotify, Apple Music, Amazon Music and Google Play) |
| | Personal music collection on CD, record or tape |
| | Music videos (i.e. music video channels or sites that you mainly use for background listening such as through YouTube or on MTV) |
| **Communicating** | Through a social networking site, e.g. Facebook, Twitter (excluding checking updates) |
| | By Instant Messaging (e.g. Facebook Messenger, WhatsApp, BBM) |
| | By email (reading or writing emails) |
| | By text message (SMS, including iMessage, reading or writing) |
| | By photo or video messages (MMS, viewing or sending) or Snapchat |
| | By phone call |
| | By video calls (including Skype, Facetime, etc.) |
| **Gaming** | Games (on an electronic device, e.g. phone, games console) |
| **Reading/browsing/using** | A newspaper/article (printed or online/digital including apps) |
| | A magazine/article (printed or online/digital including apps) |
| | Other online news, e.g. BBC News, Sky News (not through a newspaper site) |
| | Sports news/updates (not through a newspaper site) |
| | A book (printed or eBook) |
| | Online shopping or ticketing site/app |
| | Other websites or apps – including checking updates on social networks (e.g. Facebook, Twitter), online banking, etc. |
| | Other activities such as creating office documents/spreadsheets, creating or editing videos/music/audio, etc. or other apps or software/programs |

Likewise, some activities, perhaps also like listening and watching, are likely to be done simultaneously with other pursuits. The radio may be on, for instance, whilst a child is playing in their bedroom or chatting with their parents in the car. Whereas other media activities, like gaming, are more likely to absorb the majority of a child's attention span. In some ways, we may be able to make a link between the extent to which a form of media activity is a solo or group pastime, or the extent to which it is something that engages a child fully or is a background feature, and whether it is more of a **passive** or **active** form of media usage. We will be coming back to these terms in just a moment.

## 'Passive' and 'active' media activities

In this book we are predominantly going to be thinking about what children are watching, how they are communicating, what they are playing and what they are browsing and doing online. Some of the examples we will be looking at can be considered to be 'traditional' or 'broadcast' media (Reid Chassiakos et al., 2016), such as television and film viewing and listening to the radio. Some of them can be categorised as 'digital media', which includes 'applications (apps), multiplayer video games, YouTube videos, or video blogs (vlogs)' (Reid Chassiakos et al., 2016, p. e2). And within digital media falls 'social media', in which children are able to socialise and interact with other people through websites and apps like Facebook and Instagram. Traditional or broadcast media is often seen to be a **passive** activity, in which children sit and absorb content. In contrast, digital and social media usage is a more **active** endeavour, in which children engage in sharing, creating and interacting with content. Thus, the image of a child as a 'couch potato' who mindlessly receives content (perhaps akin to the myth of children as 'empty vessels') is perhaps now a little outdated as children, although predominantly sedentary, are not simply receivers but creators and curators of content too.

This shift towards the active nature of media mirrors the change in how children are viewed. Jones (2009, p. 30) describes how traditionally children have been seen as passive and incapable, whereas there is an emerging view of children as active and capable. Similarly, James and Prout (2003, p. 8) describe the emergent paradigm as viewing children as active agents in their own lives rather than the 'passive subjects of social structures and processes' that they may typically have been perceived as (James and Prout, 2003, p. 8). Essentially, what this may suggest is that as the way in which children are seen has changed, so has the way that children are expected, permitted and facilitated to engage with types of media activity. This is something we will come back to later in this chapter and also in Chapter 6 (*Children as consumers: The impact of advertising*).

## Time to consider

Table 2.1 shows 28 types of media activity and communications, which were all tracked as part of Ofcom's *Digital Day* (2016a). In the next section of this chapter we will be looking at this study in more detail. Before we do, we would like you to think about these activities and do the following three things:

1. Estimate what percentage of children aged 6–11 engage in each of the five overarching categories (watching, listening, communicating, playing, and reading/browsing/using).
2. Guess which 3 of the 28 activities were undertaken by the largest percentage of children.
3. Guess which 3 of the 28 activities were undertaken by the smallest percentage of children.

## What do we know about children's media use in the UK?

Whatever age you are, we imagine that one thing each of our readers will argue is 'children spend more time using media than when I was a child'. And, whatever age you are, we imagine you are probably right. A brilliant source of information for statistics on children's media use in the UK is Ofcom. Ofcom stands for 'the Office of Communications' and is the UK's regulator of communication services. Communication services cover areas such as television, radio, broadband, phone networks and even the postal service. As of February 2020, Ofcom now also holds the position of 'online harms regulator', which means it is responsible for keeping children safe online by ensuring that websites where users are able to share content (such as videos, comments or in forums) remove illegal content (such as child abuse images) quickly. We will be talking about this more in Chapter 4 (*Viewing violence: Just a moral panic?*).

Every year Ofcom publishes two important reports on children and parents' media use. The first of these is called 'Children and Parents: Media Use and Attitudes', of which the latest publication focuses on data from 2019 (Ofcom, 2020a). This report collected data from 3,243 interviews focusing on children aged 3–15 (Ofcom, 2020b). For children aged 3–7, 1,664 interviews took place with parents about their children's media access and these parents' attitudes to their media use and what measures they put in place to restrict and monitor it. In addition, 2,343 interviews took place with children aged between 8 and 15 and their parents, in which children were asked questions about their media use and again parents were asked what they thought of their children's media use and how they limited it. The research had some interesting findings. For instance, it identified that 50% of ten year olds owned a mobile phone, and half of 12–15 year olds reported that they had come across hateful content online, when in

2016 only a third reported this. The most popular platform for children to access content online, which was more popular than on-demand services of television, was YouTube. Interviews with parents identified that just 55% of parents believe that the benefits of their child being online outweigh the risks, whilst this figure stood at 65% in 2015.

Whilst 'Children and Parents: Media Use and Attitudes' is a large-scale study which shares quantitative findings of children's media use, Ofcom complements this with a small-scale, longitudinal, qualitative study called 'Children's Media Lives', which is now in its sixth wave (Ofcom, 2020c). This study aims to track how the same 18 children (aged between 8 and 18) are engaging with digital media. It uses a variety of data collection methods, including interviews, observations, social media tracking and 360-degree filming, to 'capture a complete picture of their environment' and 'get beyond what children say to provide evidence of what they are actually doing' (2020c, p. 3). Significant findings from the 2019 research are that children are copying social media influencers, and some are aware of their own following, although in general children keep their online profiles minimal. As a longitudinal study, researchers have been able to identify that over time the amount of on-demand content that children are consuming has increased, and children are increasingly engaging in content alone rather than with their family.

As we said earlier, in 2016 Ofcom conducted a study called 'The Digital Day'. In this piece of research, 238 primary school children and 238 secondary school children took part in completing a three-day media diary in which they recorded how much time they spent engaging in any of 28 forms of media and communication activities. The activities were divided into four categories of watching, listening, communicating, and reading/browsing/using and the diaries were recorded on two weekdays and one weekend day. Children aged between 6 and 11 spent on average 4 hours 49 minutes engaging with forms of media and communication, whilst children aged 11–15 had an average use of 6 hours 20 minutes. This illustrates that children are spending a large proportion of their waking hours not in school, consuming, creating and communicating using digital devices, and thus demonstrates why it is crucial we consider what impacts this may be having on their learning, development and socialisation.

And finally, in the last *Time to consider* we asked you to estimate what percentage of children aged 6–11 engaged in each of the five overarching categories. The study found that over the three-day period, of children aged 6 to 11:

- 98% engaged in a 'watching' activity
- 91% engaged in a 'playing' activity
- 80% engaged in a 'reading/browsing/using' activity
- 59% engaged in a 'listening' activity
- 30% engaged in a 'communication' activity

The three individual activities which were undertaken by the largest percentage of primary school-aged children were: playing video games (81%), watching live TV (80%) and reading books (print or digital) (62%). The three activities that were undertaken by the smallest percentage of children were: reading newspapers (print or digital) (1%), emailing (1%) and reading other online news (2%).

### Time to consider

Ofcom's (2016a) *Digital Day* study did not just have child participants, it had adult participants too, who also carried out an audit of their media use. Like the children, they had to record how much time they spent on a variety of digital media use activities, recorded in minutes. We would like to encourage you to do the same. Make a note of how long you spend doing the following things over the next 24 hours:

- Watching television
- Browsing the internet (on any device)
- Making phone calls, video calls and messaging
- Playing on video games
- Listening to the radio

After you have done that, we would like you to guesstimate how much time you might have spent on the same activities when you were a child. Are the amounts similar or different to how much time children in the twenty-first century are spending on media use? If you think children now spend more time than you did, what do you think you might have been doing instead?

## How has children's media use changed over time?

### During the twenty-first century

Something that stands out from reading Ofcom's (2020a, 2020c) reports is that children's media use is changing rapidly. What is good about both Ofcom's 'Children and Parents: Media Use and Attitudes' and 'Children's Media Lives' studies is that they have both been running for a number of years, so readers are able to see the extent to which children's media use has changed over the past few years, as Table 2.2 illustrates by comparing data from two of Ofcom's reports (2014, 2020a).

However, because advances in children's media use are happening so quickly, older pieces of research by Ofcom do not always capture the same data as newer ones. For instance, whilst Ofcom's 2014 study notes what percentage of children have a television in their bedroom (19% of 3–4 year olds and 35% of 5–7 year olds), this information is not seen as significant in the 2019 findings, which instead report that 15% of 3–4 year olds and 14% of 5–7 year olds are able to take a

**TABLE 2.2** Children's media use in 2014 and 2019

| | 3–4 years old | | 5–7 years old | |
|---|---|---|---|---|
| | **2014** | **2019** | **2014** | **2019** |
| Tablet ownership (%) | 11 | 24 | 23 | 37 |
| Watching on-demand services (%) | 15 | 65 | 28 | 73 |
| Children who have a social media profile (%) | 2 | 1 | 5 | 4 |
| Amount of weekly hours watching TV (hours) | 14 | 12hr 42 | 13.3 | 11hr 6 |
| Amount of weekly hours gaming (hours) | 6.1 | **4hr 42** | **6.8** | 6hr 18 |

tablet to bed with them. Similarly, whilst the 2014 findings do not report YouTube access for children aged under 8, the 2019 study reports that 3–7 year olds were watching on average between eight and nine hours of YouTube per week.

## During the twentieth century

And it is important to consider not just children's media use in the twenty-first century, but before this as well. As we said earlier in this chapter, historically children's media use has focused on 'traditional' or 'broadcast' media, such as television and radio programmes. A brilliant source of information about children's historic media use comes from Paik (2001) who has written a history of children's use of electronic media. A limitation of the chapter for a UK audience is that Paik is writing from a US perspective, yet still the source shares some valuable information about the development of film, radio, television and computer-based media. For instance, when we think of children's engagement with electronic media, we may think of it being a relatively new experience. Yet Paik (2001, p. 9) says that the average US child was attending the cinema 1.6 times a week in 1929, and when colour feature-length animated films began to be shown (the first of which was Disney's *Snow White and the Seven Dwarfs* in 1937), this appealed to large family audiences. Similarly, the first radio programmes specifically aimed at children began to be produced in the late 1920s, and by the mid-1930s US 9–12 year olds were listening to the radio between two and three hours a day (DeBoer, 1937; Jersild, 1939, cited in Paik, 2001). Paik also notes how both cinema trips and radio consumption were adversely affected by the rise in television ownership in the 1950s, during which time a 'children's hour' was introduced between 5:30 and 6:30pm which showed television programmes specifically aimed at young children.

Historical film, radio and television use is similar in the UK to the US. In the UK, radio programmes for children began in 1922 with *Children's Hour*, which was broadcast on BBC radio until 1964. The first television programmes for children began in 1937 with *For the Children*, which, for instance, would include presenters reading stories such as those by Hans Christian Andersen. The programme was suspended during World War Two but made a return in 1946 with the puppet *Muffin the Mule* and ran until 1964. In 1950 the BBC's Children's Television Department was established, and programmes such as *Andy Pandy*, *The Flowerpot Men* and *Rag, Tag and Bobtail* were commissioned and eventually broadcast under the title of 'Watch with Mother' (Holmes, 2016). Despite *Andy Pandy* only enjoying an original run from 1950 to 1970, in 2002 a stop motion version was produced and shown on CBeebies, the BBC's channel for pre-school children, showing the enduring appeal of the characters. Similarly, in 2001 a revival of *The Flowerpot Men*, entitled *Bill and Ben*, was also created for CBeebies, almost 50 years after the original run from 1952 to 1954. Then, throughout the 1950s more children's programmes began to be commissioned, including *Blue Peter*, which is the longest-running children's television programme in the world, with the first episode broadcast in 1958.

Even from the 1950s producers recognised the ability of pre-school children's television programmes to provide education. Holmes (2016) talks about how one early BBC pre-school programme, *Play School*, was designed following the consideration of early years pioneers like Fredrich Froebel, and was marketed by the BBC as being 'a response to poor nursery provision in the 1960s' (2016, p. 36), as nurseries which had opened to facilitate women working during World War Two were shut down. We will be talking more about *Play School* in Chapter 3 (*Children's media as education, not entertainment*).

### Time to consider

In the next few chapters we will be considering what some of the positive and negative impacts of children's media use are considered to be. Have a look at Table 2.1 and think about what Ofcom (2020a) is telling us about children's media usage and think about what the implications of this might be.

## What are the contexts of children's media use?

As well as considering what children's media use is, and how it has changed over time, we need to think about *where* children's media use is taking place. In Chapter 8 (*Helpful theoretical lenses: How theory can help us understand children's engagement with the media*) we will think in more detail about children's contexts in relation to theory such as Bronfenbrenner's ecological systems model, but for now it is worth starting by considering just a couple of the contexts in a child's microsystem – their home and their ECEC setting – and thinking about what children's media use looks like in those environments.

## Children's media use in the home

We have already thought in this chapter about children's media use in the home, but what we have not touched upon is the changing nature of children's media usage as a solitary activity in the home, when traditionally families have taken part in mass media consumption together, for instance when watching television or listening to the radio. However, children are now engaging in an increasing amount of active media consumption alone in their bedrooms. In 2007, 69% of children aged 5–15 had a television in their bedroom, including around a fifth of 3–4 year olds and just over a half of 5–7 year olds (Ofcom, 2016b). By 2017, the percentage of children aged 5 to 15 with a television in their bedroom had fallen to 48%. Yet, as you may have guessed, this is not because the trend for children to consume media alone is declining. As we said earlier, in 2019, 15% of 3–4 year olds and 14% of 5–7 year olds were allowed to take a tablet to bed with them (Ofcom, 2020a). This jumps to 32% of 8–11 year olds, 45% of whom are also allowed to take their mobile phone to bed with them.

This is significant because there is the potential that parents are becoming less aware of the intricacies of how much time their children are spending online, and what they are doing online. In 2019 the UK's Chief Medical Officers published a report which offered eight pieces of advice to parents about children's screen and social media usage (Davies et al., 2019). One of their recommendations was that, for the purpose of good quality sleep, mobile phones should be left outside the bedroom when it is time for bed. Other organisations promote internet use taking place outside of the bedroom for other reasons. For instance, the BBC (2021) recommends that parents always sit with young children when they are using the internet. Internet Matters (2021) suggests to parents that they 'encourage [their children] to use devices in the same room as you so you can keep an eye on how they're using the internet'.

However, Livingstone et al. (2017) argue that parents are becoming savvier to the notion that children need support and that they should be monitoring their child's internet use. They cite a survey by Lupiáñez-Villanueva et al. (2016) which found that over 80% of UK parents of 6–14 year olds reported their children used the internet in a public room at home, in comparison to just over half of parents who said their children could access the internet in their own room. As Livingstone et al. (2017) note, it is important to remember that in this study data was gathered via parental reports about their children's internet usage, and indeed parents might not always know the full picture of when their children are spending time online.

## Children's media use in ECEC settings

Meanwhile, media use in early childhood settings is likely to look quite different from that in the home environment. A revised Statutory Framework for the Early Years Foundation Stage (EYFS) came into force in England in September 2021, with seven areas of learning and development. One of these areas is

'Understanding the World', which involves 'guiding children to make sense of their physical world and their community' and fostering children's 'understanding of our culturally, socially, technologically and ecologically diverse world' (DfE, 2021b, p. 10). The previous Statutory Framework for the EYFS (DfE, 2017) contained an Early Learning Goal for Technology, that 'children recognise that a range of technology is used in places such as homes and schools. They select and use technology for particular purposes' (DfE, 2017, p. 12). No corresponding goal is present in the 2021 revised Statutory Framework, which seems odd given the growing role that media and electronic technology play in children's lives.

The DfE have provided non-statutory curriculum guidance to accompany the Statutory Framework (DfE, 2021a), although references to children's electronic media use are limited. For instance, one suggestion is that babies, toddlers and young children use computers or tablets to develop their mark-making skills (DfE, 2021a, p. 117), whilst another is that practitioners 'provide appropriate non-fiction books and links to information online to help [children] follow their interests' (2021a, p. 15). Meanwhile, the Early Years Coalition's non-statutory guidance for the EYFS, 'Birth to Five', billed as being 'guidance for the sector, by the sector' and lauded by practitioners, notes that there is not an Early Learning Goal for Technology but still contains a section of guidance to support technology development. Their own Early Learning Goal for Technology states:

> Children require access to a range of technologies, both digital and non-digital in their early lives. Exploring with different technologies through play provides opportunities to develop skills that children will go on to develop in their lifetimes. Investigations, scientific inquiry and exploration are essential components of learning about and with technology both digitally and in the natural world. Through technology children have additional opportunities to learn across all areas in both formal and informal ways. Technologies should be seen as tools to learn both from and with, in order to integrate technology effectively within early years practice.
>
> (Early Education, 2021, p. 112)

Before we go any further, it is also important to note that although the above quotation appears to be from Early Education (2021), the document itself is a reworking of *Development Matters* (Early Education, 2012) by a group of practitioners, consultants and academics, which was then proposed to the ECEC sector, who then commented on it before the final draft was published by Early Education in 2021. The commitment to supporting children's technological development within this non-statutory guidance demonstrates that even within children's earliest years, they are able and should be supported to develop the capabilities and competences to help them take advantage of technological tools and practices. In a divided society where not all children will have access to the same types of digital technologies at home due to what can be prohibitive costs, providing these in early years settings can ensure that all children are able to have the opportunity to engage with them.

**TABLE 2.3** Reflecting on the removal of the Technology ELG in the Statutory Framework for the Early Years Foundation Stage (DfE, 2021)

| Reasons the Technology ELG should have been removed | Reasons the Technology ELG should not have been removed |
|---|---|
| *For example: Digital technologies can be expensive for early childhood settings with limited budgets.*<br>*For example: Some educational philosophies, such as the Steiner-Waldorf philosophy, do not advocate digital technology use in early childhood.* | *For example: Digital technologies are an increasingly large part of children's lives so children should have the opportunity to learn how to use them safely and appropriately.* |

## Time to consider

It is time to think critically about the removal of an Early Learning Goal about technology in the revised EYFS (DfE, 2021). Why do you think it might have been removed? What do you think it says that the ECEC sector have written their own Early Learning Goal (ELG) about technology in their non-statutory 'Birth to Five' guidance? Do you think it should have been removed? Completing a table like Table 2.3 may help you decide.

## Final reflection

As children's media usage is increasing, so is the importance of thinking critically about what the implications of this use might be. There are considered to be a variety of positive impacts of children's engagement with media, such as the potential for academic benefits, and negative impacts, such as on children's mental health, which this book will go on to think about in the coming chapters. However, it is incorrect to believe that children's media use is a new phenomenon, as actually children's engagement with digital media dates back to the 1920s. Unlike back in the 1920s, children are able to engage with digital technologies in a wide range of contexts, including in their homes and early years settings.

## Key points

- It is important to consider children's engagement with digital media as it can have a profound impact (both positive and negative) on their lives.
- Children's media usage is rising. For instance, in 2019, 24% of 3–4 year olds had their own tablet, up from 11% in 2014. This illustrates why we should be giving our attention to how children use and engage with types of media.
- Children's media usage is not something new; children's radio programmes have been broadcast since the 1920s and children's television programmes have been broadcast in the UK since the 1930s.
- There are several different contexts of children's media use, including their homes and early years settings.

## Further reading

1. Paik, H. (2001) 'The History of Children's Use of Electronic Media', in D.G. Singer and J.L. Singer (eds), *Handbook of Children and the Media*. London: Sage, pp. 7–27.This is a chapter by Paik which gives an overview of the history of children's use of electronic media in the US. The point of this chapter is to illustrate that children's engagement with electronic media is not a new phenomenon, but has been increasing since the 1920s.
2. Ofcom (2020) 'Children and Parents: Media Use and Attitudes Research Project'. Available at: www.ofcom.org.uk/__data/assets/pdf_file/0023/190616/children-media-use-attitudes-2019-report.pdf (accessed 4 March 2020).Every year Ofcom publish the findings of their 'Children and Parents: Media Use and Attitudes' research project. It shows us what children's media use is like, what parents and children think about their media use and how parents regulate it. The most recent report is from 2020 and presents findings from the 2019 round of data collection. You can use it to compare twenty-first-century UK children's media engagement with how Paik (2001) describes media engagement historically.
3. Holmes, S. (2016) 'Revisiting Play School: A Historical Case Study of the BBC's Address to the Pre-School Audience', *Journal of Popular Television*, 4(1), pp. 29–47. Whilst Paik (2001) is writing about children's historic media use from a US perspective, Holmes shares a case study of one BBC programme aimed at pre-schoolers, *Play School*, which ran between 1964 and 1988. She discusses what it says about the BBC's view of the needs of pre-school children, their attempts to draw upon early years pioneers like Friedrich Froebel when designing the programme, and the way in which it was seen as a 'form of televisual nursery in an environment where external facilities were sparse' (p. 37).

## References

BBC (2021) *Keeping Children Safe Online*. Available at: www.bbc.co.uk/cbeebies/grownups/article-internet-use-and-safety (accessed 29 August 2021).

Davies, S.C., Atherton F., Calderwood C. and McBride M. (2019) *United Kingdom Chief Medical Officers' commentary on screen-based activities and children and young people's mental health and psychosocial wellbeing: a systematic map of reviews*. Department of Health and Social Care. Available at: https://assets.publishing.service.gov.uk/government/uploads/system/uploads/attachment_data/file/777026/UK_CMO_commentary_on_screentime_and_social_media_map_of_reviews.pdf (accessed 29 August 2021).

Department for Education (DfE) (2017) *Statutory Framework for the Early Years Foundation Stage*. Available at: https://assets.publishing.service.gov.uk/government/uploads/system/uploads/attachment_data/file/596629/EYFS_STATUTORY_FRAMEWORK_2017.pdf (accessed 29 August 2021).

Department for Education (2021a) *Development Matters*. Available at: https://assets.publishing.service.gov.uk/government/uploads/system/uploads/attachment_data/file/1007446/6.7534_DfE_Development_Matters_Report_and_illustrations_web__2_.pdf (accessed 29 October 2021).

Department for Education (2021b) *Statutory Framework for the Early Years Foundation Stage*. Available at: https://assets.publishing.service.gov.uk/government/uploads/system/uploads/attachment_data/file/974907/EYFS_framework_-_March_2021.pdf (accessed 29 August 2021).

Early Education (2012) *Development Matters*. Available at: www.foundationyears.org.uk/files/2012/03/Development-Matters-FINAL-PRINT-AMENDED.pdf (accessed 29 August 2021).

Early Education (2021) *Birth to 5 Matters: Non-Statutory Guidance for the Early Years Foundation Stage*. Available at: www.birthto5matters.org.uk/wp-content/uploads/2021/04/Birthto5 Matters-download.pdf (accessed 29 August 2021).

Holmes, S. (2016) 'Revisiting Play School: A Historical Case Study of the BBC's Address to the Pre-School Audience', *Journal of Popular Television*, 4(1), pp. 29–47.

Internet Matters (2021) *Preschool (0–5) Online Safety Advice*. Available at: www.internetmatters.org/advice/0-5/ (accessed 29 August 2021).

James, A. and Prout, A. (2003) *Constructing and Reconstructing Childhood*. London: Falmer Press.

Jones, P. (2009) *Rethinking Childhood*. London: Continuum.

Livingstone, S., Davidson, J., Bryce, J. and Batool, S. (2017) *Children's Online Activities, Risks and Safety: A Literature Review by the UKCCIS Evidence Group*. Available at: www.lse.ac.uk/business-and-consultancy/consulting/assets/documents/childrens-online-activities-risks-and-safety.pdf (accessed 29 August 2021).

Ofcom (2014) *Children and Parents: Media Use and Attitudes Report*. Available at: www.ofcom.org.uk/__data/assets/pdf_file/0027/76266/childrens_2014_report.pdf (accessed 29 August 2021).

Ofcom (2016a) *Digital Day 2016*. Available at: www.ofcom.org.uk/__data/assets/pdf_file/0017/94013/Childrens-Digital Day-report-2016.pdf (accessed 29 August 2021).

Ofcom (2016b) *Children and Parents: Media Use and Attitudes Report*. Available at: www.ofcom.org.uk/__data/assets/pdf_file/0034/93976/Children-Parents-Media-Use-Attitudes-Report-2016.pdf (accessed 29 August 2021).

Ofcom (2020a) *Children and Parents: Media Use and Attitudes Report 2019*. Available at: www.ofcom.org.uk/__data/assets/pdf_file/0023/190616/children-media-use-attitudes-2019-report.pdf (accessed 29 August 2021).

Ofcom (2020b) *Ofcom's Children's Media Literacy 2019 Technical Report*. Available at: www.ofcom.org.uk/__data/assets/pdf file/0016/161701/childrens-media-use-attitudes-2019-technical-report.pdf (accessed 29 August 2021).

Ofcom (2020c) *Children' Media Lives – Wave 6*. Available at: www.ofcom.org.uk/__data/assets/pdf_file/0021/190524/cml-year-6-findings.pdf (accessed 29 August 2021).

Paik, H. (2001) 'The History of Children's Use of Electronic Media', in D.G. Singer and J.L Singer (eds), *Handbook of Children and the Media*. London: Sage, pp. 7–27.

Reid Chassiakos, Y., Radesky, J., Christakis, D., Moreno, M.A. and Cross, C. (2016) 'Children and Adolescents and Digital Media', *Pediatrics*, 38(5). DOI: https://doi.org/10.1542/peds.2016-2593.

CHAPTER

3

# Children's media as education, not entertainment

When you think about children using forms of electronic media, like watching television or playing on a tablet, what do you think the purpose of this is? Often when we think about children's media usage, we believe that they are engaging with types of media (or being allowed by their parents to engage) predominantly for the purpose of entertainment. Moreover, many people think that media use has a detrimental impact on children's academic attainment, because children, for instance, watch television or play video games in lieu of doing their homework or more educationally beneficial activities. However, there are many different types of media interactions that can provide educational benefits for children, such as educational pre-school television programmes and touchscreen apps; this chapter is going to focus on these forms of media.

In this chapter we are going to consider the role that media usage, in particular television and tablet use, plays in supporting children's learning and development. We will consider the three facets of the reduction hypothesis (Shin, 2004, cited in Kirsh, 2010), which posits that there is a correlation between excessive media use and poor educational attainment, and assess the evidence for this hypothesis. We will take *Sesame Street* as an example of a children's television programme that provides pre-school children with learning opportunities (Mares and Pan, 2013). We will also explore claims made about touchscreen use (Bedford et al., 2016; AAP, 2016). Finally, we will consider how sometimes the educational benefits of children's digital activities are overlooked by parents and schools (Chaudron, 2015).

## In what ways can media engagement support children's learning?

We are going to start this chapter by thinking about the ways that media engagement can support children's learning. Can you think about how this might hap-

 DOI: 10.4324/9781003121206-4

pen? Would you say that media engagement has ever supported your learning? In what ways? One programme, *Sesame Street*, which we'll talk about in more detail in a moment, has been found to have facilitated learning outcomes not only in relation to 'traditional' pre-school content such as numbers, letters and shapes, but also in terms of learning about the world and about prosocial behaviours (Mares and Pan, 2013). And many other programmes offer similar benefits, too. So, although many assume that children's media usage has a negative impact on children's academic and educational attainment, there is in fact evidence that media use can provide positive benefits on children's developmental outcomes. We know from Chapter 2 (*Children's media lives*) that 'media engagement' is a broad term and encompasses a lot of different types of media usage. In this section we are going to think about two different types of media – television viewing and using touchscreens.

## Watching television

We considered in Chapter 2 (*Children's media lives*) that children have been watching television for many years; we also introduced an article by Holmes (2016), who talks about *Play School*, a children's television programme that aired on the BBC between 1964 and 1988. She talks about the significance of the name of the programme itself; *Play School* was originally set to be called *Home School*, however Holmes (2016, p. 33) notes that 'the change [in name] speaks to a wider historical narrative in which the BBC have always claimed that the purpose of their children's output is primarily recreational and not educational'. Essentially, this suggests that the BBC do firmly view their children's media programmes, both on television and radio, as entertainment rather than education. Yet despite the overarching focus being recreation, the aims of the programme were also to 'offer some of the experience that a good nursery school can provide' (Felgate, 1973, cited in Holmes, 2016, p. 34). With this in mind, the programme included what was termed by the creators as 'hard work' for the child viewers to engage with, such as learning numbers and letters. It also used expertise from external educational advisors to support the educational offerings, in a similar way to children's television programmes today. For instance, the CBeebies offering *Bing*, which first aired in 2014, was created in conjunction with '23 external writers, two Montessori teachers, four educational advisers and a speech and language therapist' (Mance, 2020). Other CBeebies television programmes such as *Teletubbies* 'are similarly built on educationalists' insights into what a particular age group can handle' (Mance, 2020).

### Teletubbies

Holmes (2016, p. 30) mentions that within the British context, little focus has been given to individual pre-school television programmes, with a few exceptions, one being *Teletubbies*. From a UK perspective, *Teletubbies* is one of the most famous programmes currently broadcast for babies and young children. It was originally broadcast between 1997 and 2001 and then revived in 2015. When the programme was restarted, the BBC (2015) described it as 'one of the most successful global children's programmes of all time', and said that the original series had been seen by over a billion children, in over 120 territories in 45 different languages. Notably, it was the first western pre-school children's television programme to be broadcast in China, watched by 300 million children there (BBC, 2015). It was also sold to the US's Public Broadcasting System (PBS) despite 'a scarcity of children's programmes from other countries on U.S. screens' (Buckingham, 1998, p. 292). Yet, is there research to suggest it is beneficial for young children to watch *Teletubbies*? Findings about the benefits of the programme are mixed. Pempek et al. (2010) conducted an experiment where children between 6 and 24 months old were shown normal and distorted versions of the programme. They found that until children reach around 18 months, 'it remains to be determined what, if anything, infants comprehend in commercial infant-directed videos', and therefore 'if there is, in fact, little comprehension, then the time spent watching television may well be time better spent engaged in other activities such as toy play' (p. 1292).

Yet Marsh's (2000) study with slightly older children, aged 3 and 4, found that using *Teletubbies* as a stimulus in literacy activities in an early years setting created a shared discourse and shared understandings between children, and supported their reading, writing and oral work. The child participants did not actually watch *Teletubbies* as part of the study, so the study can be questioned on its inclusivity towards participants who may not have watched *Teletubbies* at home. Instead, they took part in activities related to the programme, like making and eating Tubby custard (the staple food for Teletubbies) as well as reading and making Teletubbies comics. Marsh (2000) considers how the children talked about the programme in relation to their home lives (like what merchandise they had or who their favourite character was), which gave them an opportunity to demonstrate their cultural capital, which is a term we will consider more in Chapter 8 (*Helpful theoretical lenses: How theory can help us understand children's engagement with the media*), and perhaps their family's economic capital too. Marsh states that such an opportunity for children 'provides a means of locating new understandings within a familiar discourse' (p. 130), and for the particular participants in this study, 'the Teletubbies created opportunities for learning to be situated in a comfortable landscape and enabled them to integrate home experiences with schooled literacy' (ibid.). We should, however, consider this in relation to the commercialisation of childhood, something we will consider in Chapter 6 (*Children as consumers: The impact of advertising*). Using *Teletubbies* as a stimulus for discussion and activities in ECEC settings may increase children's 'pester power' towards *Teletubbies* merchandise, sales of which reportedly generated £1 billion between 1997 and 2000 (Jones, 2002).

Meanwhile Buckingham (1998) theorises as to why adults like us might like the programme and why, in relation to the original run at least, it developed a cult following: perhaps because adults might see it as a form of 'regression' or because the Teletubbies could be seen as 'a necessary process of recovering childlike pleasures – in silly noises and games, in anarchy and absurdity, for which irony provides a convenient alibi' (p. 293). It is, of course, relevant to remember that pre-school children are introduced to programming predominantly through their parents and those in their microsystems (see Chapter 8: *Helpful theoretical lenses: How theory can help us understand children's engagement with the media*), so appealing to adults, as well as children, is key to a pre-school programme's success.

## Sesame Street

From a US perspective, one example of a television programme famed for supporting children's learning is *Sesame Street*. First broadcast in 1969, *Sesame Street* combines live action with puppetry with the aim of supporting children's learning, especially children from low-income households. It was developed against the social backdrop of the Civil Rights movement of the 1950s and 1960s and the creation of the Head Start programme (launched in 1965), both of which recognised the 'crucial role education would have to play if children from low-income circumstances, including disproportionately large numbers of minority-group members, were to escape the cycle of poverty' (Palmer and Fisch, 2001, p. 4). Like *Play School* and *Bing*, a firm staple of the *Sesame Street* team since its inception has been educational advisors and researchers supporting the development of content; the creators wanted a children's television programme that would combine education and entertainment. It has continued to have a detailed curriculum and incorporates educational goals such as literacy, numeracy, prosocial behaviours and understanding the world. This means that from the beginning it has 'responded to the need for early childhood education' (ibid.). It also supports children to understand topical global events, such as a piece in June 2020 where the father of Elmo, one of the puppet characters, explains to him why the Black Lives Matter protests were taking place.

Whilst early years education is commonplace in many parts of the world, there are still countries, particularly in the poorest areas of the world, with low rates of pre-school attendance. *Sesame Street* has been seen as a way to counter the lack of early years settings in some of these countries and is believed to act as a 'major early education intervention' (Mares and Pan, 2013, p. 40) in place of pre-school enrolment. As of 2013, the programme was broadcast in over 130 countries. And although not all children in those countries will have access to television, or electricity, many will: in a 2008 Indian survey 58% of children had access to television, of which just over a fifth had watched the Indian version of *Sesame Street*, *Galli Galli Sim Sim*, in the week prior to responding (GyanVriksh Technologies, 2008, cited in Mares and Pan, 2013). Unlike other programmes which are simply dubbed into the local language, instead many international co-productions of *Sesame Street* are produced (Mares and Pan, 2013). These co-productions work with local educational specialists to respond to particular educational goals for the relevant country and develop sets, characters and live-action videos that will be relevant to the audience: for instance, responding to particular health challenges like HIV/AIDS in South Africa, or portraying both Catholic and Protestant traditions in a positive light in Northern Ireland.

In 2013, Mares and Pan (2013) conducted a meta-analysis of 21 pieces of research about *Sesame Street* that focus on the educational impact of the programme outside of the US. The authors were interested in *Sesame Street* as a form of informal education, particularly in low-income regions that do not have the funding or means to provide formal early childhood development and care. The study aimed to answer two research questions: first, whether there are positive effects of watching *Sesame Street* outside of the US; and secondly, whether the programme had more success teaching some types of educational content than other types. With this in mind, Mares and Pan broke down types of learning into three broad categories – cognitive outcomes, learning about the world, and social reasoning and attitudes.

The study certainly has some limitations – some of the publications analysed are particularly old, with the oldest piece of research dating back to 1972, and some may be critiqued with regard to their objectivity as they are themselves internal *Sesame Street* reports. But the findings suggest that:

> across 24 studies conducted with more than 10,000 children from 15 countries, those who watched more performed better than those who watched less … watching Sesame Street was associated with learning about letters, numbers, shapes, and sizes – the elements of basic literacy and numeracy that remain fraught for millions of children globally. It was also associated with learning about science, the environment, one's culture, and health and safety-related practices such as washing one's hands or wearing a bike helmet. Finally, it was also associated with more prosocial reasoning about social interactions and more positive attitudes toward various out-groups, including those that were associated with long-standing hostilities or stereotyping.
>
> (Mares and Pan, 2013, p. 148)

What Mares and Pan (2013) aren't suggesting is that watching programmes like *Sesame Street* can replace attending an ECEC setting; but what they *are* suggesting is that *Sesame Street* is watched by millions of children worldwide who otherwise would not have access to an educational curriculum and, for those children, there are positive benefits. Is this something that surprises you?

## Time to consider

Imagine you are responsible for creating a co-production of *Sesame Street* for your particular locality. You have to make a pitch to producers about what you think the programme should address. Think about these questions to help you write your pitch:

- What are relevant local issues that you would want to address? These could be related to social matters or health and safety practices, for instance.

- What areas of the early years curriculum would you want the programme to focus on? This could be, for instance, personal, social, and emotional development, language, mathematics, understanding the world, or something else.
- What characters, sets and props would you have, so that your local audience can relate to the programme?

## Tablet and touchscreen use

Another type of media use that has been found to have a positive impact on children's learning and development is touchscreen use. Bedford et al. (2016) suggest that, although parents have concerns about the impact of touchscreen use on their children's attainment (as we will talk about in the next section), it is hard to find evidence to support this. The researchers have established the TABLET (Toddler Attentional Behaviours and LEarning with Touchscreens) project to examine how engagement with touchscreens is impacting on the social, cognitive and brain development of children aged between 6 months and 3 years (Cinelab, 2021). Early findings from the research project explored the link between touchscreen use and meeting milestones in gross motor development (sitting and walking), fine motor development (demonstrating pincer grip and stacking blocks) and language development (uttering first word and combining two words). They found there was no significant relationship between using touchscreens and language development or gross motor development. However, touchscreen use was linked with earlier fine motor development. The findings suggest that earlier touchscreen use, specifically the age at which children begin scrolling rather than simply watching videos, is associated with an earlier ability to stack blocks.

Since this piece of research was published, Bedford et al. have conducted other studies to examine the impact of tablet and touchscreen use. One later study has found that toddlers with high touchscreen use found it harder to complete a screen-based task without avoiding distractions from new images appearing on the screen (Portugal et al., 2021a). Does this apply to you, too? How distracted are you by adverts and notifications that pop up on the screen? Although you might think that having your attention diverted by something new on the screen is disadvantageous, Portugal, Bedford and Smith (2021b) do point out that there are situations where this could be valuable, such as when spotting abnormalities on airport security screens or in air traffic control.

The benefits of touchscreen use are sometimes overlooked by organisations who publish guidance for parents on what media activities children should be engaging with, and for how long. One of these organisations is the American Academy of Pediatrics (AAP), who published a policy statement in 2016 setting out to paediatricians, families and industry how young children's media use should be managed. They suggest that paediatricians need to guide families in areas such as 'creating unplugged spaces and times in their homes' and 'the

**TABLE 3.1** Recommendations for young children's digital screen use

| Audience | Guidelines |
|---|---|
| Paediatricians | |
| Families | |
| Industry | |

ability of new technologies to be used in social and creative ways' (AAP, 2016, p. 3). Although they suggest that there can be educational benefits of touch-screen use for young children, such as learning new words, overall the AAP recommend that digital media use should be avoided for children younger than 18–24 months old because of the clinical implications for areas such as obesity and sleep, with the exception of video calls (AAP, 2016, p. 3). This may be of some relief to those parenting in the Covid-19 pandemic, whose children are likely to have increased the amount of time spent on video calls with extended family whilst they were restricted from seeing them face-to-face.

## Time to consider

The AAP (2016) has published recommendations for paediatricians, families and industry to help them manage children's digital screen time. For instance:

- For paediatricians: 'Educate parents about brain development in the early years and the importance of hands-on, unstructured, and social play to build language, cognitive, and social-emotional skills' (AAP, 2016, p. 3).
- Families: 'Do not feel pressured to introduce technology early; interfaces are so intuitive that children will figure them out quickly once they start using them at home or in school' (AAP, 2016, p. 3).
- Industry: 'Make high-quality products accessible and affordable to low-income families and in multiple languages' (AAP, 2016, p. 4).

If you were responsible for setting guidelines like the AAP (2016), what would you include? Complete Table 3.1 below to help you think about what your recommendations would be.

## What are the myths around media engagement and poor educational attainment?

Despite the evidence of the benefits of children's media engagement, there are also views that media usage has a negative impact on children's academic attainment. For instance, the AAP (2016, p. 3) argues that paediatric providers must inform parents of 'the importance of not displacing sleep, exercise, play, reading aloud, and social interactions' with digital media. This idea of media use displacing other activities is one of the hypotheses explored in a piece of research by Shin (2004). He set out to explore some 'reduction hypotheses' about the impact of media engagement (specifically watching television) on children's academic attainment. The reduction hypothesis 'contends that excessive media consumption leads to poor academic performance' (Kirsh, 2010, p. 42). Shin argues that there are three hypothetical models that fit with the reduction hypothesis (a) the time-displacement hypothesis, (b) the mental effort-passivity hypothesis, and (c) the attention-arousal hypothesis.

## Shin's (2004) reduction hypotheses

The *time-displacement* hypothesis is the idea that because of media engagement, like video games, listening to music and watching television, children spend less time doing activities that are related to educational endeavours, like doing their homework. The *mental effort-passivity* hypothesis argues that as a result of engaging with media use, children become mentally lazy. This is because, Shin suggests, watching television is a relatively passive activity and this makes children less invested and less willing to do more intellectually challenging activities such as reading. It also posits that because it is easier to absorb the information from television than it is from an activity like reading, television programmes are faster paced and this hinders children's reflective thinking, as the speed of television programmes means that children do not have the chance to reflect (Valenburg and van der Voort, 1994, cited in Shin, 2004). Finally, the *attention-arousal* hypothesis posits that (a) watching television can have a negative impact on children's attention spans, which may lead to difficulties concentrating on academic tasks, and (b) watching television may arouse the viewer and lead to impulsive behaviours, which again are not conducive to concentrating on academic tasks.

In Shin's research exploring the behaviours of just over 1,200 children, he found that the more time children watched television, the less time they spent doing homework, studying and reading for leisure, and they therefore had lower levels of academic achievement. At the same time, parents reported more instances of impulsive behaviour in their children the more time they spent watching television. Shin therefore argues that his data supports the three hypotheses. But what do you think of Shin's findings? They may support what you already think about the impact of media use on children' academic achievement. But if we think critically about these findings, an obvious downside to Shin's research is the date of the publication; it was published in 2004 and used data from a 1997 longitudinal study. A lot has changed in terms of children's television viewing habits since then. In addition, we do not know what types of programmes the children were watching. And finally, we know that in 2022 television viewing makes up only one part of children's media usage.

**TABLE 3.2** Hypotheses about the impact of media use

| Hypothesis | Definition | Evidence |
|---|---|---|
| Time-displacement hypothesis | | |
| Mental effort- passivity hypothesis | | |
| Attention-arousal hypothesis | | |
| Stimulation hypothesis | | |

## Kirsh's (2010) critique of Shin (2004)

In 2010, Kirsh (2010) critiqued Shin's (2004) study and found that for each of the three hypotheses, there is little empirical evidence to support it. Again, it is important to remember that over ten years has passed since Kirsh made this claim. Yet in relation to the *time-displacement* hypothesis, he explains that rather than displace educational activities, media use tends to displace other forms of media use, or other forms of leisure activities. In relation to the *mental effort-passivity* hypothesis, Kirsh argues that 'when consuming screen media, children are cognitively active' (Kirsh, 2010, p. 43), evidenced by the fact that they ask questions about the media they are consuming and the discussions they have about it. Finally, in relation to the *impulsivity* hypothesis, Kirsh suggests that there is no data to support this theory and it is instead just a myth. Instead, Kirsh shares evidence that supports a *stimulation* hypothesis, which is 'that media use fuels the brain, resulting in greater academic achievement' (Kirsh, 2010, p. 45). Certainly we have considered so far in this chapter that watching educational programmes such as *Sesame Street* may have a positive impact on academic achievement, rather than a negative impact as Shin's three reduction hypotheses would suggest. We might suppose that Shin's hypotheses are part of a *moral panic* about children's media use, something that we will consider more in Chapter 4 (*Viewing violence: Just a moral panic?*).

## Time to consider

It can be tricky to get your head around the three reduction hypotheses explored by Shin (2004) and also Kirsh's (2010) stimulation hypothesis. Take a moment to write your own definitions of them in Table 3.2. Then, spend some time considering what evidence you know of to support or refute each claim.

## Are the benefits of children's media usage overlooked?

We can see from the guidelines given about children's media usage by the American Academy of Pediatrics (2016), as well as the reduction hypotheses proposed by Shin (2004), that there are reasons why parents and educators may be wary of supporting young children's media engagement. But the danger of this attitude is that the positive benefits of children's media usage might be overlooked. This is something that Blum-Ross and Livingstone (2016) consider. They mapped the advice on screen time given to parents from 23 different organisations, including from UK government and regulatory bodies, industry, non-governmental organisations, the press and the media. They found that, on the whole, the advice was focused more towards the risks rather than the rewards that media engagement can offer. The implication of this is that 'advice focused on risk mainly advocates that parents employ restrictive mediation strategies whereas opportunity-focused advice mainly emphasises active mediation' (Blum-Ross and Livingstone, 2016, p. 13). Different types of sources employ different attitudes towards the risk and opportunities of screen time. For example, all but one suggest some form of social restriction is necessary, such as screen time limits and rules on what websites can be accessed, whereas less than half advocate computing and browser restrictions such as parental controls and Wi-Fi time limit access. Advice from government and regulatory bodies is the most likely to emphasis the risks, but only five of the 23 organisations stressed that 'children's use of digital media need not be all negative, that the role of parents extends beyond limiting and restricting, and that the difficult task is therefore to judge, and to balance, media-related opportunities and risks' (ibid.).

Similarly, Chaudron (2015, p. 8) also notes that the 'benefits of the children's digital activities are less straightforward to parents than seeing the risks and reside in fostering creativity, imagination, social skills, knowledge acquisition, hand-eye coordination and educational provision for future'. His research also suggests that while some parents are aware of how digital media use can lead to benefits in relation to areas such as hand–eye coordination and knowledge acquisition, other parents need more support about what websites or online games they should be encouraging and how as parents they should be mediating their children's digital use. With this in mind he recommends:

- Development and promotion of information materials outlining the positive benefits of engagement with digital technology, with a focus on positive content, educational, creative, communication and social outcomes.
- Encouragement for schools to take a more active role in promoting creative and educational uses of digital technologies as well as addressing safety matters at home with parents and carers.

(Chaudron, 2015, p. 8)

## Time to consider

Think about Chaudron's (2015) first recommendation that information materials should be developed and promoted. Choose an audience, such as parents, educators or policy makers, and design a poster to inform them of the positive benefits of digital technologies. You may wish to just focus on one type of positive outcome (educational, creative, communication or social) of engaging with digital technologies, or you might want to choose more than one.

## Final reflection

In this chapter we have thought about the tension that exists between media usage for the purpose of education and that for the purpose of entertainment. We have considered whether it is possible for media engagement in relation to activities like watching television or using touchscreens to have cognitive benefits. We have also considered how in the absence of early years education, whether internationally (Mares and Pan, 2013) or historically (Holmes, 2016), high-quality children's television programmes can provide educational benefits for children. We have also explored how earlier touchscreen use can lead to the earlier development of fine motor skills, and support children's skills in recognising new stimuli on the screen. Yet despite these positive impacts, still myths and moral panic exist about the detrimental impact of children's media use on academic attainment, for instance as highlighted by the hypotheses developed by Shin (2004). These myths, alongside a focus on the risks of media usage being prevalent in guidance for parents and educators, mean that the educational value of digital technologies is often overlooked (Chaudron, 2015). Those working with young children should aim to ensure that families are aware of the positive benefits that engaging with certain types of media can bring, in relation to children's educational, creative, communication and social outcomes.

## Key points

- There are several television programmes that aim to have educational benefits for young children, such as *Sesame Street*, *Teletubbies* and *Play School*.
- Early touchscreen use has been found to correlate with meeting fine motor milestones earlier. Also, children with high levels of touchscreen use find it harder to avoid distractions on screen.
- There are several hypotheses of the impact of media use, including the time-displacement hypothesis, the mental effort-passivity hypothesis, the attention-arousal hypothesis and the stimulation hypothesis.
- We must ensure that parents and educators are supported to understand the educational value of digital technologies, and do not solely focus on the risks that media engagement can bring.

## Further reading

1. Mares, M. and Pan, Z. (2013) 'Effects of Sesame Street: A Meta-Analysis of Children's Learning in 15 Countries', *Journal of Applied Developmental*

*Psychology*, 34(3), pp. 140–151. In this piece of research Mares and Pan (2013) examined 24 studies that had explored whether in non-US contexts there were positive effects of watching *Sesame Street* for children. When you read it, be wary that many of the studies they cite were originally internal reports commissioned by the *Sesame Street* production company and in consultation with their staff, so they may have a particularly vested interest in proclaiming the benefits of the programme. However, this means the authors had access to data not previously published.

2. Holdsworth, A. (2015) 'Something Special: Care, Pre-School Television and the Dis/Abled Child', *The Journal of Popular Television*, 3(2), pp. 163–178. Whilst Mares and Pan (2013) are writing about a US television programme, Holdsworth is writing about the UK pre-school television programme *Something Special*, which was originally commissioned for children with special educational needs. It's a fascinating read about the programme and 'the implicit and explicit rhetorics of "care" within the remit and content of the UK pre-school children's channel CBeebies' (2015, p. 163).

## References


American Academy of Pediatrics (2016) 'Media and Young Minds: Council on Communications and Media', *Pediatrics*, 135(4): e20162591. DOI: 10.1542/peds.2016-2591.

BBC (2015) *Teletubbies*. Available at: www.bbc.co.uk/mediacentre/mediapacks/teletubbies (accessed 30 August 2021).

Bedford, R., Saez de Urabain, I., Cheung, C.H.M., Karmiloff-Smith, A., and Smith, T.J. (2016) 'Toddlers' Fine Motor Milestone Achievement Is Associated with Early Touchscreen Scrolling', *Frontiers in Psychology*, 7. doi.org/10.3389/fpsyg.2016.01108.

Blum-Ross, A. and Livingstone, S. (2016) *Families and Screen Time: Current Advice and Emerging Research*. Available at: http://eprints.lse.ac.uk/66927/1/Policy%20Brief%2017-%20Families%20%20Screen%20Time.pdf (accessed 7 July 2021).

Buckingham, D. (1998) 'Re-Viewing Our Media Childhoods', *Journal of Adolescent & Adult Literacy*, 42(4), pp. 292–294.

Chaudron, S. (2015) *Young Children (0–8) and Digital Technology*. Available at: www.lse.ac.uk/media@lse/research/ToddlersAndTablets/RelevantPublications/Young-Children-(0-8)-and-Digital-Technology.pdf (accessed 7 July 2021)

Cinelab (2021) *Tablet Project*. Available at: www.cinelabresearch.com/tablet-project (accessed 30 August 2021).

Fisch, S.M. and Truglio, R.T. (eds) (2001) *'G' Is for Growing: Thirty Years of Research on Children and Sesame Street*. Mahwah, NJ: Routledge.

Holmes, S. (2016) 'Revisiting Play School: A Historical Case Study of the BBC's Address to the Pre-School Audience', *Journal of Popular Television*, 4(1), pp. 29–47.

Jones, T. (2002) *Innovating at the Edge: How Organizations Evolve and Embed Innovation Capability*. London: Routledge.

Kirsh, S.J. (2010) *Media and Youth: A Developmental Perspective*. Chichester: Wiley-Blackwell.

Mance, H. (2020) 'How Much TV Should Your Children Be Watching Right Now?', Financial Times, 9 April.

Mares, M. and Pan, Z. (2013) 'Effects of Sesame Street: A Meta-Analysis of Children's Learning in 15 Countries', *Journal of Applied Developmental Psychology*, 34, pp. 140–151.

Marsh, J. (2000) 'Teletubby Tales: Popular Culture in the Early Years Language and Literacy Curriculum', *Contemporary Issues in Early Childhood*, 1(2), pp. 119–133.

Palmer, E.L. and Fisch, S.M. (2001) 'The Beginnings of *Sesame Street* Research', in S.M. Fisch and R.T. Truglio (eds), *'G' Is for Growing: Thirty Years of Research on Children and 'Sesame Street'*, Mahwah, NJ: Routledge, pp. 3–24.

Pempek, T.A., Kirkorian, H.L., Richards, J.E., Anderson, D.R., Lund, A.F. and Stevens, M. (2010) 'Video Comprehensibility and Attention in Very Young Children', *Developmental Psychology*, 45(5), pp. 1283–1293.

Portugal, A.M., Bedford, R., Cheung, C.H.M., Mason, L. and Smith, T.J. (2021a) 'Longitudinal Touchscreen Use across Early Development Is Associated with Faster Exogenous and Reduced Endogenous Attention Control', *Scientific Reports*, 11, 2205. DOI: https://doi.org/10.1038/s41598-021-81775-7.

Portugal, A.M., Bedford, R. and Smith, T.J. (2021b) *Touchscreens May Make Toddlers More Distractible – New Three-Year Study*. Available at: https://theconversation.com/touchscreens-may-make-toddlers-more-distractible-new-three-year-study-154036 (accessed 30 August 2021).

Shin, N. (2004) 'Exploring Pathways from Television Viewing to Academic Achievement in School Age Children', *The Journal of Genetic Psychology*, 165(4), pp. 367–382.

CHAPTER

4

# Viewing violence

## Just a moral panic?

This chapter will begin by examining the moral panic (Cohen, 1971) around children's media usage (Critcher, 2008; Livingstone, 2009), and explore whether we are primed to fear new types of media, dating back to Plato's concerns that the written word would create forgetfulness in learners and more recent concerns that violent games contribute to a violent society (Messenger Davies, 2010). We will then explore what some of the negative impacts of viewing media violence are deemed to be (Kirsh, 2006), make links to social learning theory, and critique Bandura's (1961) classic Bobo doll experiment. We will go on to talk about measures like the watershed that have been put in place to shield children from accessing violent content. We will also assess the role of factual and evaluative mediation (Nathanson, 2004) in supporting children to understand violent materials.

## Are we primed to fear new types of media?

You are probably aware that often adults have concerns about children's media use. There are fears that their digital media usage has a negative impact on academic achievement, leads to poor mental health, limits outdoor play and opens children up to online stranger danger. In Chapter 3 (*Children's media as education, not entertainment*) we also thought about how there are myths around how watching television could make children mentally lazy, impact on their attention spans and lead to them spending less time doing educational activities (Shin, 2004). However, some would argue that these concerns are unfounded, in fact simply a *moral panic*.

### Moral panics

You might not have come across the term 'moral panic' before. Scott (2014, p. 492) defines it as:

> the process of arousing social concern of an issue – usually the work of moral entrepreneurs and the mass media. The concept was used most forcefully

DOI: 10.4324/9781003121206-5

> by Stanley Cohen in *Folks Devils and Moral Panics* (1971), with reference to the concern of the teenage styles of Mods and Rockers in England in the mid-1960s, but it has since been applied in the analysis of the societal reaction to many other social problems, including football hooliganism, child abuse, AIDS, and numerous subcultural activities.

If there is a moral panic about something, then that means there is a widespread belief, which is misguided, false or exaggerated, that something is a threat to a community's or society's values. A moral panic about children's media usage is the exaggerated or irrational idea that children engaging in certain media activities will be detrimental to the norms of society.

You might think that the moral panic around media use is a relatively new thing, but in fact Messenger Davies (2010) tracks it all the way back to Plato, who lived in Athens between 429 and 347 BCE. He stated that the discovery of the written word would 'create forgetfulness in the learners' souls, because they will not use their memories' (Messenger Davies, 2010, p. 75). More recently, and specifically to children's media use, Messenger Davies (2010, p. 76) highlights that back in the 1930s, *The Christian Century* argued that 'the movies are so occupied with crime and sex stuff and are so saturating the minds of children the world over with social sewage that they have become a menace to the mental and moral life of the coming generation'. Similar claims were made about films, comic books, television and video games throughout the twentieth century, with Livingstone arguing that

> the moral panics associated with the arrival of each new medium, which demand that research addresses the same questions over and again – about the displacement of reading, exercise and conversation, about social isolation and addiction, about violent and consumerist content ... – have a long history.
>
> (Livingstone, 2009, p. 152)

This demonstrates how a fear about children's media engagement is not a new phenomenon but dates back thousands of years. Yet Springhall (1998, p. 7) argues that the response to each new moral panic is the same:

> we can expect a campaign by adults to regulate, ban or censor, followed by a lessening of interest until the appearance of a new medium reopens public debate. Each new panic develops as if it were the first time ... and yet the debates are strikingly similar.

In the UK, part of the moral panic around media usage has focused specifically on 'video nasties'. First used in an article in the *Sunday Times* in 1982, the term describes uncensored home video horror films that 'dwell on murder, multiple rape, butchery, sadomasochism, mutilation of women, cannibalism and Nazi atrocities' (Chippendale, 1982). This was followed by a campaign led by Mary Whitehouse to regulate and control the distribution of these videos, which fuelled a moral panic about them and their 'associations with danger and corruption of children', later described as 'absurd' (Barker, 2020, p. 29). Hours after the Hungerford and Dunblane massacres, video nasties were said to be responsible for the killers' motives, before there had been time for any possible link to be investigated (Petley, 2012). They were also blamed for the actions of the perpetrators of the murder of 2-year-old James Bulger, although it was disputed in court whether violent films had influenced James Bulger's killers (Kirby, 1993). Nevertheless, following the case of James Bulger, new legislation was put in place in the UK around video films, demonstrating the power of moral panics and the fear they can generate.

## Time to consider

The concept of moral panics can be tricky to get your head around. Take some time to think about what a moral panic is. Now think about why moral panics in relation to media use might develop.

## The Bobo doll experiments

Part of the reason for a moral panic around children's television viewing is because of research conducted by Albert Bandura and his colleagues. In 1961, Bandura, Ross and Ross (1961) published a piece of research which has become famously known as 'the Bobo doll experiment' (a Bobo doll is a 1.5m inflatable doll that is weighted at the bottom, so that when hit, it returns to standing). The research sought to investigate whether when children witnessed aggressive and violent acts, they would imitate them. Thus, 36 girls and 36 boys aged between 3 and 5 were divided into eight groups. Children from four of the groups individually witnessed an adult (in some cases of the same sex as the child, and in some cases of the opposite sex) behave aggressively towards the Bobo doll. Children from the remaining groups witnessed an adult (again either of the same or opposite sex) play with other non-violent toys. After observing this, each child was taken to a test room which contained toys that could be used in typically aggressive play (such as a smaller Bobo doll and dart guns) and toys typically not used in an aggressive fashion (like crayons and paper, teddy bears and small world toys). The children were then observed playing over a 20-minute period to see how they interacted and played with the toys on offer.

The findings of the research were that the children who had been exposed to the adult acting aggressively to the Bobo doll were much more likely to behave aggressively to the doll themselves. Both boys and girls were likely to imitate a male adult behaving aggressively more than a female adult, but were more likely to imitate verbal aggression having observed an adult of the same sex as them. The study demonstrates that children are likely to imitate aggressive behaviour that they have witnessed.

Bandura, Ross and Ross followed this up in 1963 with an experiment which considered the extent to which children would imitate aggressive behaviour that they witnessed on screen, rather than in real life. In this study, 48 boys and 48 girls aged between 3 and 5 were divided into four groups. Children in the first group witnessed an adult behaving aggressively towards a Bobo doll, as in their 1961 experiment. Children in the second group watched a film recording of the adult behaving in the same way. The third group watched a film featuring a cartoon cat called Herman who also used a Bobo doll aggressively. The final group was a control group who did not observe anything but were themselves observed in the test room. As in the 1961 experiment, each child was taken to the test room, which had a variety of toys typically used in an aggressive and non-aggressive way, to be observed for a 20-minute period.

The main findings of this second study

> provide strong evidence that exposure to filmed aggression heightens aggressive reactions in children. Subjects who viewed the aggressive human and cartoon models on film exhibited nearly twice as much aggression as did subjects in the control group who were not exposed to the aggressive film content.
> (Bandura, Ross and Ross, 1963, p. 9)

In fact, all the subjects who witnessed aggression, whether in real life or on film, displayed more aggressive behaviour than the control group during observation. The implication of this, Bandura and his colleagues suggest, is that 'pictorial mass media, particularly television, may serve as an important source of social behaviour (ibid.). This experiment has been extensively used as evidence of the impact of children watching violent and aggressive television programmes worldwide.

Yet Messenger Davies (2010, p. 82) critiques Bandura's experiment, stating

> in raising questions over the uncritical way in which this research has been so widely reported, I am not defending explicit and gruesome violence in entertainment material offered to children ... I would be only too happy for someone to come up with some really conclusive evidence about the harmful effects of violence ... but this has not been produced.

She has concerns that the results of the experiment do not support the way in which the findings have been interpreted and extrapolated to imply that the main reason for aggression in children is that they have witnessed aggression on television. Messenger Davies also has concerns about the use of experimental research to determine the effects of media usage, as 'experiments are artificial; they do not measure long-term influence; they tend to be carried out on very unrepresentative groups of children' (2010, pp. 8–9).

## Time to consider

You might already have been familiar with the Bobo doll experiments (in fact, Messenger Davies (2010, p. 79) suggests that 'even in students who appeared not to have read anything else, the Bobo doll experiment was the one that everyone was able to describe'). Messenger Davies advocates thinking critically about the studies rather than taking them, and their reported findings, at face value. In our experience with students, Bandura et al.'s studies are often ones that students write and talk about having read secondary sources about the experiments, rather than the original sources. We would encourage you to find and read the original journal articles so you can come to your own conclusions and critique about them. Here are the references:

Bandura, A., Ross, D. and Ross, S.A. (1961) 'Transmission of Aggression through the Imitation of Aggressive Models', *Journal of Abnormal and Social Psychology*, 63(3), pp. 575–582.

Bandura, A., Ross, D. and Ross, S.A. (1963) 'Imitation of Film-Mediated Aggressive Models', *Journal of Abnormal and Social Psychology*, 66(1), pp. 3–11.

## What is said to be the impact of media violence?

### Viewing violent television content

As we spoke about earlier in this chapter, experimental research on the effects of media violence on television is often critiqued because it cannot measure long-term effects of viewing aggressive and violent content. But two of the long-term impacts may be a *habituation to media violence* and a *desensitisation to real-world violence*. Kirsh notes that sometimes these two terms are conflated and that it is important to distinguish between the two. He states:

- *The habituation to media violence effect* refers to a decreased level of responsiveness to *media* violence as a result of repeated viewing of violent *media* images' (2006, p. 220).
- The *desensitization to real-world violence effect* refers to a decreased level of responsiveness to *real-world* violence as a result of repeated exposure to *media* violence' (2006, p. 220).

Kirsh suggests that it is important to recognise the difference between these two effects because the impact of them can be quite different; the habituation effect simply suggests that children become less responsive to violence that they watch on screen, whereas the desensitisation effect could lead to children being less receptive to violence that they see in real life, and also, Kirsh (2006, p. 221) argues, 'more likely to engage in violent behaviour themselves'. Earlier in this chapter we thought about the moral panic around video nasties, and in particular the belief that they can lead to a desensitisation to real-world violence, as suggested in relation to the motive of James Bulger's murder. Kirsh (2006, p. 221) suggests there is evidence that viewing violent television can cause behavioural, physiological, cognitive and emotional desensitisation, though caveats this with the fact that there is a paucity of research in this area.

Kirsh (2006) also argues that several different factors may influence the impact of viewing violent content, for instance, whether it is watched at the cinema or on television at home. Take a moment to think about this: which one do you think is more likely to have a greater effect on children? Kirsh states that some research shows that viewers are more likely to recall scenes they viewed on a larger screen, and such scenes may also generate a larger physiological response (Reeves et al., 1999, cited in Kirsh, 2006; Heo, 2004, cited in Kirsh, 2006). However, on the other hand, he suggests that when television programmes have adverts, a commercial break between a violent act and the punishment of that act can mean that children do not make the link of there being a negative consequence for the aggression action, so are more likely to act in a violent way themselves (Collins, 1973, cited in Kirsh, 2006). Yet this point does need to be considered within a twenty-first-century context. With multiple on-demand platforms and facilities to fast-forward advertisements, children may be less likely to experience a break between a violent act and the repercussions of it, thus minimising the chance that children will not be able to take on board any anti-aggressive messages. We will think more about the impact of advertising on children in Chapter 6 (*Children as consumers: The impact of advertising*).

## Playing violent video games

We considered in Chapter 2 (*Children's media lives*) how the amount of time children spend watching television is decreasing, but other media habits, such as playing video games, are increasing. Another facet of the moral panic around children's media use is concern around the impact of playing violent video games. In relation to this, the evidence is mixed. On the one hand, some studies demonstrate that there is a link between playing violent video games and displaying aggressive behaviour (Milani et al., 2015); however, some of this demonstrates **correlation** between playing video games and level of aggression, rather than evidence that playing video games **causes** aggressive behaviour. Meanwhile, in one longitudinal study, violent gaming was not found to have a negative impact on children aged 7–11 displaying externalising behaviours (i.e. behaviours that are anti-social, violent or aggressive) or on their propensity to demonstrate prosocial behaviour (Lobel et al., 2017). Children took part in two interviews one year apart, and the study did find that at the second interview point, the number of children who expressed an interest in violent video games had increased by 50%. The researchers consider whether this may be because violent games become more interesting to children as they grow up, as the games begin to grapple with more mature themes and often are themselves more challenging and complex as they are aimed at an older audience. This suggests that violent video games do not have an impact on children's aggressive and anti-social behaviour.

In fact, one study has demonstrated that playing *Fortnite*, described as a violent game, may actually increase children's prosocial behaviour (Shoshani and Krauskopf, 2021). Child participants aged 9 to 12 were split into groups to play a violent game (*Fortnite*) or a neutral game (a pinball arcade game), either alone or co-operatively (i.e. with a partner). They were then asked to complete some tasks designed to assess their levels of helpful behaviour. The study found that children were more likely to be helpful if they had been playing with a partner, and also that children were more likely to be helpful if they had been playing the violent game rather than the neutral game. The authors state that the research

> contributes to the growing number of studies that challenge the common assumption that violent video games lead directly to a decrease in prosocial behavior. These results emphasize the importance of the context of the game, not just the content, when examining the effects of video games on social behavior.
>
> (2021, p. 7).

They stress the 'social paradox' of online video games, in which although adults may worry that playing video games may increase social isolation, instead children are able to virtually socialise and interact with others from around the world. This may be particularly important for those with additional needs who face barriers to meeting friends face-to-face. We can consider how much of this parental worry about social isolation comes about as a result of the moral panic around children's media use that, ironically, the media itself fuels.

Others, too, have noted the moral panic around video game use, such as Ferguson (2015) who talks about how links were made between video game use and the actions of the perpetrator of the Sandy Hook massacre before any official data about his media use history were examined. In his meta-analysis of studies linking video game use (both violent and non-violent) to children's levels of aggression, wellbeing, prosocial behaviour and academic attainment, Ferguson found that there may be a minimal link between use and increased aggression and poor mental health alongside decreased academic outcomes and prosocial behaviour. Yet there are often limitations in the research design of studies with these findings. For instance, in experimental research, often violent and non-violent games are compared which are mismatched in terms of things like competitiveness and difficulty. Pretests on participants are not routinely done to examine the impact of playing a violent or non-violent video game on aggression levels. Sometimes studies do not control for variables such as gender, family violence and trait aggression (i.e. how likely a person is to respond to situations in an aggressive manner). Other studies selectively interpret their findings, or are selective in which other studies they cite, focusing on those which support their own hypotheses. There is ambiguity too around what constitutes a violent video game; one testifying psychologist in a murder trial stated that even *Pac Man* could be deemed violent (Rushton, 2013, cited in Ferguson, 2015, p. 657). Ferguson suggests that these limitations are 'systemic throughout the field' (2015, p. 649); thus, we should approach studies that examine video games and the outcomes on children and adolescents with caution.

## Time to consider

Shoshani and Krauskopf (2021, p. 8) suggest that

> parents, educators, researchers and the general public should become more familiar with today's video games, understand them, explore the risks and opportunities that they have for children, and leverage these to connect children to each other, foster their prosocial behavior and self-esteem, emphasize their character strengths, and promote their healthy and positive development.

Think about this quotation in relation to the following questions:

- How do you think parents and educators could be encouraged to take time to become more familiar with today's video games?
- What do you think are the barriers that stop adults becoming more familiar at the moment?
- The authors talk about 'leveraging' the opportunities of video games, i.e. taking maximum advantage of them. What do you think are some of the ways they might be able to do this?

## How can children be protected from unsuitable violent content?

### The watershed

In the UK, measures are in place to limit children's exposure to inappropriate television content, although the effectiveness of them can be debated. Since 1964 terrestrial television channels have had a 'watershed' of 9pm; before this time there are rules in place about what can be broadcast (Ofcom, 2021). However, we can critique the effectiveness of a 'watershed' in a world where increasingly children access television programmes on their tablets and phones rather than on television sets themselves, and where many programmes can be accessed via on-demand or catch-up services at any time of day. As we mentioned in Chapter 2 (*Children's media lives*), in 2020 Ofcom also became the UK's 'online harms regulator', which means that as well as taking responsibility for maintaining the watershed on television, they now also hold responsibility for tackling harmful content online, including on video sharing platforms founded in the UK (Ofcom, 2020). This hopefully means that children will be less likely to come across violent content and other content that is unsuitable for them. Perhaps this new role as online harms regulator is now more important than maintaining the watershed, as children spend more time online and less time watching television.

Ofcom (2021) argue that the watershed is still important, as it 'continues to help parents protect their children from material that might be unsuitable or even harmful for them' (Ofcom, 2021). They state that they conduct research twice a year to ascertain adults' views about the watershed, with 74% of the general public and 76% of parents specifically thinking that 9pm is the right time. In 2014, they also conducted research to explore audience attitudes towards violent content on television (Ofcom, 2014). In the study, both parents and non-parents believed that the reason for regulating violent content on television should be to safeguard and protect children. They found parents had different views on children viewing violent content dependent on the age of the child. For primary-aged children they focused on protecting their children, whereas for secondary-aged children their emphasis changed to 'preparing children for the world and their more independent life within it' (Ofcom, 2014, p. 27). This meant that parents were more likely to let their secondary-aged children watch violent content (with the exception of violent content of a sexual nature). This was due to the fact that older children were seen by parents to have a greater ability to understand that programmes on television are not real life, and also to have a greater ability to process what they had watched.

## Mediating children's television viewing

To support children to better understand violent television content, adults can *mediate* children's television viewing, which means they can act as an intermediator (i.e. a go-between) between their children and the television programme to help them to understand it. Nathanson (2004) conducted experimental research that explored which of two types of mediation was more effective in mediating children's violent television viewing: 123 children were split into three groups, who received factual mediation, evaluative mediation, or no mediation, respectively, after watching the same clip of a live-action programme of superheroes being violent towards their enemies. In the factual mediation approach, the adult spoke to the children about how the programme was produced, such as 'Those people in the TV show are just actors playing a part' (2004, p. 326). Essentially, the adult was giving **facts** about how the programme was made, to support children to distinguish it from real life. In the evaluative mediation approach, children were instead told negative evaluations of the characters, such as 'All of those people in the TV show are NOT cool. Even the guys in the masks aren't cool. Nobody likes people who act like they do' (ibid.). The adult was sharing their **evaluations** and assessments of the characters, based upon their violent behaviour. The final group did not receive any mediation at all. Following this, children completed a questionnaire containing questions about their attitudes to the clip, including questions about what they thought about the protagonists and whether they thought the violence they had witnessed was justified. Nathanson found that evaluative mediation was more effective, especially amongst younger children aged 5 to 7, in reducing unwanted outcomes from watching violent content. She also found that factual mediation was not successful, and in some instances, particularly with older children aged 12 to 15 who do not normally watch violent television programmes already, it may be damaging to them as it may encourage them to consider this genre that they may have previously overlooked or not been interested in.

## Time to consider

This research suggests that evaluative mediation is a more effective strategy than factual mediation for parents, teachers and early years practitioners to use to help children process and make sense of violent television content. Imagine you were sitting down with a child or group of children to watch some children's television that contained some violent content. It might be something aimed at children, like a cartoon (such as *Tom and Jerry*) or a scene from a Disney film (such as the townspeople's attack on the Beast in *Beauty and the Beast*). Or it might be something that children had come across that their parents were watching, like a soap (Ofcom's (2014) research showed participants pre-watershed violent clips from *Eastenders*, *Emmerdale* and *Hollyoaks*). Reflect upon the things you might say to support the children in evaluating the way in which the characters are behaving. Sentences starting with phrases like this may help you:

- This character is making me feel … (i.e. evaluative mediation)
- I am concerned by … (i.e. evaluative mediation)
- I'm interested in finding out how … (i.e. factual mediation)
- The acting/set/props look … (i.e. factual mediation)

## Final reflection

In this chapter we have explored the idea of media use and media violence and the potential impact on children. We have considered whether concern about media use is simply a moral panic, as people such as Livingstone (2009) and Messenger Davies (2010) would argue, or whether there is evidence to suggest that media use is dangerous and damaging to children. We have examined research by Bandura, Ross and Ross (1961, 1963) that has had a significant impact on how children viewing violence on screen is perceived, despite limitations to the experiments and the way they have subsequently been reported by secondary sources (Messenger Davies, 2010). We have also explored similar limitations around research examining violent video games (Ferguson, 2015). We have also looked at what the evidence is of the impact of media violence on children (Kirsh, 2006) and explored strategies such as evaluative and factual mediation (Nathanson, 2004) that may support children who watch violent media content.

## Key points

- Since the discovery of the written word there have been *moral panics* around media use, because of fears that it will lead to issues such as the 'dumbing down' of society, and laziness, addiction, isolation or violent tendencies in children.
- There is evidence that watching violence and aggression on screen can lead to children imitating this (Bandura, Ross and Ross, 1961, 1963) and also evidence that watching violent content can have desensitisation effects on a child's behaviours, physiology, cognition and emotions (Kirsh, 2006).
- Many studies that have examined the link between violence and video games (both violent and non-violent games) have limitations to the research design. Common limitations are due to mismatched violent and non-violent games being compared; a failure to pretest participants; a failure to account for other variables; and a failure to be clear on what constitutes 'violence' in a video game (Ferguson, 2015).
- As well as regulation to restrict children's access to violent media sources, factual and evaluative mediation can be effective in supporting children to understand content they watch (Nathanson, 2004).

## Further reading

1. Messenger Davies. M. (2010) *Children, Media and Culture*. Maidenhead: Open University Press. The whole of this book is useful for information about the role of media in children's lives and it's a nice accessible read. For more information about the history of moral panics around media and for Messenger Davies' critique of Bandura's experiments, have a look at Chapter 5, 'Children and Childhood in Media Studies'.
2. Adachi, P.J.C. and Willoughby, T. (2017) 'The Link between Playing Video Games and Positive Youth Outcomes', *Child Development Perspectives*, 11(3), pp. 202–206. This journal article is an interesting review of research that has been conducted to examine links between video game playing (not necessarily violent video games) and positive outcomes such as problem-solving skills, physical activity and improved mental wellbeing. We will come back to this article in Chapter 5 (*Media and children's health*) too.

## References

Bandura, A., Ross, D. and Ross, S.A. (1961) 'Transmission of Aggression through the Imitation of Aggressive Models', *Journal of Abnormal and Social Psychology*, 63(3), pp. 575–582.

Bandura, A., Ross, D. and Ross, S.A. (1963) 'Imitation of Film-Mediated Aggressive Models', *Journal of Abnormal and Social Psychology*, 66(1), pp. 3–11.

Barker, M. (2020) 'The UK "Video Nasties" Campaign Revisited: Panics, Claims-Making, Risks, and Politics', in L. Tsaliki and D. Chronaki (eds), *Discourses of Anxiety over Childhood and Youth across Cultures*. Cham, Switzerland: Palgrave Macmillan, pp. 29–50.

Chippendale, P. (1982) 'How High Street Horror Is Invading the Home', *The Sunday Times*, 23 May.

Cohen, S. (1971) *Folk Devils and Moral Panics*. London: Routledge.

Critcher, C. (2008) 'Moral Panic Analysis: Past, Present, Future', *Sociology Compass*, 2(4), pp. 1127–1144.

Ferguson, C.J. (2015) 'Do Angry Birds Make for Angry Children? A Meta-Analysis of Video Game Influences on Children's and Adolescents' Aggression, Mental Health, Prosocial Behavior, and Academic Performance', *Perspectives on Psychological Science*, 10(5), pp. 646–666.

Kirby, T. (1993) 'Video Link to Bulger Murder Disputed', *The Independent*, 26 November.

Kirsh, S.J. (2006) *Children, Adolescents and Media Violence: A Critical Look at the Research*. London: Sage.

Livingstone, S. (2009) 'Half a Century of Television in the Lives of Our Children', *The Annals of the American Academy*, 625, pp. 151–163. DOI: 10.1177/0002716209338572.

Lobel, A., Engels, R.C.M.E., Stone, L.L., Burk, W.J. and Granic, I. (2017) 'Video Gaming and Children's Psychosocial Wellbeing: A Longitudinal Study', *Journal of Youth and Adolescence*, 46, pp. 884–897.

Messenger Davies. M. (2010) *Children, Media and Culture*. Maidenhead: Open University Press.

Milani, L., Camisasca, E., Caravita, S.C.S., Ionio, C., Miragoli, S. and Di Blasio, P. (2015) 'Violent Video Games and Children's Aggressive Behaviors: An Italian Study', *SAGE Open*. DOI: 10.1177/2158244015599428.

Nathanson, A. (2004) 'Factual and Evaluative Approaches to Modifying Children's Responses to Violent Television 1', *Journal of Communication*, 54(2), pp. 321–336.

Ofcom (2014) *Audience Attitudes towards Violent Content on Television*. Available at: www.ofcom.org.uk/__data/assets/pdf_file/0024/54933/violence_on_tv_report.pdf (accessed 30 August 2021).

Ofcom (2020) *Ofcom to regulate harmful content online*. Available at: www.ofcom.org.uk/about-ofcom/latest/features-and-news/ofcom-to-regulate-harmful-content-online (accessed 30 August 2021).

Ofcom (2021) *What Is the Watershed?* Available at: www.ofcom.org.uk/tv-radio-and-on-demand/advice-for-consumers/television/what-is-the-watershed (accessed 30 August 2021).

Petley, J. (2012) '"Are We Insane?" The "Video Nasty" Moral Panic', *Recherches Sociologiques et Anthropologiques*, 43(1), pp. 35–37.

Scott, J. (2014) *A Dictionary of Sociology*. Oxford: Oxford University Press.

Shin, N. (2004) 'Exploring Pathways from Television Viewing to Academic Achievement in School Age Children', *The Journal of Genetic Psychology*, 165(4), pp. 367–382.

Shoshani, A. and Krauskopf, M. (2021) 'The Fortnite Social Paradox: The Effects of Violent-Cooperative Multi-Player Video Games on Children's Basic Psychological Needs and Prosocial Behavior', *Computers in Human Behaviour*, 116. DOI: https://doi.org/10.1016/j.chb.2020.106641.

Springhall, J. (1998) *Youth, Popular Culture and Moral Panics: Penny Gaffs to Gangsta Rap*. Basingstoke: Macmillan.

CHAPTER

# 5 Media and children's health

In this chapter we will focus on the ways in which media usage and engagement can have an impact on children's health. We will begin by looking at children's physical health; this is a timely focus as the World Health Organization (2020) recently recommended that it is necessary to 'tighten national regulation of harmful commercial marketing' as exposure to unhealthy food and drinks advertising is contributing to rising levels of obesity in children. We will look at marketing campaigns such as *Change4Life* which produces television and radio adverts and apps to create behaviour change to reduce obesity. The chapter will then consider children's mental health and look specifically at both the positive and negative impacts social media can have on children's mental health (Frith, 2017; Royal Society for Public Health, 2017). Readers will be encouraged to assess whether they believe the benefits of social media outweigh the negatives.

But before we go any further, let's begin by thinking about why the issue of media and children's health is a concern. As we spoke about in Chapter 4 (*Viewing violence: Just a moral panic?*), there has long been a moral panic about media usage and the impact on children's physical health in terms of disrupting sleep and reducing time spent being physically active. Lindon (2011) talks about how parents are blamed by the media for 'creating a generation of couch potatoes' (p. 2), which is a common stereotype of children, who it is claimed are spending too much time watching television and playing video games. More recently, concern has also spread to the impact on children and young people's mental health too. There are fears that social media in particular can exacerbate conditions such as anxiety and depression, whilst other media usage like gaming can lead to gaming addiction.

## The impact on children's physical health

In Chapter 3 (*Children's media as education, not entertainment*) we looked at guidelines written by the American Academy of Pediatrics (AAP) (2016) on media usage for under fives. Part of these guidelines cite a variety of studies that indicate the negative impact that media use can have on children's weight, sleep and development. One of the studies they cite investigated the link between television viewing habits and health outcomes (e.g. BMI, physical activity levels and

DOI: 10.4324/9781003121206-6

food intake) in children aged between 2 and 6 (Cox et al., 2013). They found there was a small link between television viewing and a child's weight, with television viewing on weekdays being linked to having a higher BMI. The researchers suggest this may be due to the sedentary nature of television viewing displacing physical activities like playing outside; it may also be due to the propensity of children to snack whilst viewing. This supports what Kirsh (2010) argues about the displacement hypothesis that we considered in Chapter 3 – that although it is a myth that media use displaces academic activities, it does displace other leisure activities, which could be physical activities like exercise and sport.

## Media usage and children's sleep

The AAP (2016) also share research showing that media usage may impact on children's sleep, which can lead to poorer physical health and mental health outcomes, difficulties with emotional regulation and behaviour, and poorer academic attainment too. Take a moment to think about why media usage may have a negative impact on a child's sleeping habits. If you think back to Chapter 1 (*Children's media lives*) we considered how in Ofcom's (2020) survey, 15% of 3–4 year olds and 14% of 5–7 year olds were allowed to take a tablet to bed with them in 2019. This jumps to 32% of 8–11 year olds, 45% of whom are also allowed to take their mobile phone to bed with them. So part of the issue lies with the fact that children are spending time on their electronic devices instead of being asleep. However, this is not the only reason. Even children who do not have access to digital devices in their bedroom may suffer from poorer sleep if they've been exposed to screen media in the evening (Vijakkhana et al., 2015, cited in AAP, 2016). This can be because of the types of programmes children may watch of an evening (particularly if it is violent content, Garrison, Liekweg and Christakis (2011) suggest).

Another reason why digital device use in the evening can impact on sleep habits is because screens emit blue light, which can deceive the brain into thinking that it is daytime, which thus means that the brain does not produce melatonin before bed. Melatonin is a hormone that tells your brain when it is time to sleep and helps your body regulate its sleep–wake cycles. Hale et al. (2018) suggest that blue light from digital media may have a greater effect on children than on adults because children's pupils have a larger diameter, so children are more prone to have their melatonin production suppressed. However, other studies have found the link between children's digital media use and sleep habits to be minimal, with Przybylski (2019) finding that 'each hour devoted to digital screens was associated with 3–8 fewer minutes of nightly sleep', and 'children who complied with 2010 and 2016 American Academy of Pediatrics guidance on screen time limits reported between 20 and 26 more minutes, respectively, of nightly sleep' (p. 218). Przybylski suggests that what has a greater impact is contextual factors, for instance the need to wake up early for school, and that his findings should inform future research that takes place. This tallies with Fisher's (2019) analysis of the study. Fisher argues that it does not consider the 'physiologic drawbacks of less sleep, from decreased REM time and dreams to effects on memory formation and even threats to organ functions' (p. 2), and thus these areas still need to be investigated.

## Time to consider

Fisher (2019) suggests that parents and practitioners still need to 'let children dream' (p. 2) by putting boundaries for digital media use in place. This is despite Przbylski's (2019) finding that screen time has a very small impact on time spent asleep.

Design a leaflet for parents or ECEC practitioners to help them to understand how children's digital media use can impact on their sleep. Make sure you include some recommendations to help them put boundaries in place.

## Video games and children's physical health

Now let us consider what the link may be between video games and physical health. We introduced you to a literature review by Adachi and Willoughby (2017) in Chapter 4 (*Viewing violence: Just a moral panic?*). In that literature review, the authors consider several studies that have examined the link between playing video games and physical activity, arguing that, in some research, there is a relationship between playing active video games ('ex-ergames' (p. 204)) and increased heart rate, energy expenditure and oxygen consumption. You may be familiar with active video games offered on the Nintendo Wii Fit or Nintendo Switch, which both offer sports and exercise activities such as virtual boxing, Zumba, tennis and bowling. For instance, a meta-analysis of 51 studies found that there was a link between active video games and expending energy in participants aged between 3 and 17, although this report showed that active video games 'do not make a significant contribution to enable children and youth to meet guidelines of 60 minutes of moderate- to vigorous-intensity physical activity on a daily basis', and it is unknown whether these video games can instil long-term changes in players (LeBlanc et al., 2013). Similarly, Adachi and Willoughby (2017) cite Peng, Lin and Crouse (2011), whose research suggests active video games 'are effective technologies that may facilitate light- to moderate-intensity physical activity promotion' (p. 681). However, in research where children aged between 9 and 12 were given a Nintendo Wii console and either two active video games or two inactive video games, the findings suggest there was no difference in the activity levels of the two groups of children at any time (Baranowski et al., 2012).

Adachi and Willoughby (2017) also suggest that the video game *Pokémon Go* may be credited with encouraging physical exercise in children, yet at the time of writing we were yet to find studies examining this. Since their publication, there has been research that has found that the mobile game can increase activity levels, including one study by Lindqvist et al. (2018) which collected data through focus groups with parents and their children aged 7 to 12. They found that the game did promote everyday physical activity, with children encouraging their parents to join them on walks, and parents encouraging their children to play, with some walking for hundreds of kilometres. However, for these habits to be adopted long-term, the game may have to evolve with new characters or features, as 'the increased physical activity evidenced in this study remains largely dependent on the game and is therefore not likely sustainable'.

## Can media usage influence positive healthy habits?

### Change4Life

What you may be thinking is, if we know that children and their parents are spending time watching television and browsing online, perhaps we could take advantage of this to spread information about healthy habits. You may already be familiar with one such campaign, called *Change4Life*, which has been described as 'a wide range of high profile activities across different platforms, including traditional forms of advertising on television and billboards, digital communications, relationship marketing and stakeholder engagement via events and tutorials, and has been addressed to a variety of social groups' (Coleman, 2016, p. 177).

*Change4Life* launched in 2009 and has been described as a *social marketing campaign*. Sometimes people think that 'social marketing' is linked to social media in some way, but in fact the 'social' refers to the notion that the marketing is aimed at developing or improving *society*, rather than referring to the platform on which the marketing is taking place. Thus, it is a discipline of marketing aimed at promoting particular behaviours that are for social good, described by Kotler, Lee and Rothschild (2006, cited in Kotler and Lee, 2008) as 'a process that applies marketing principles and techniques to create, communicate, and deliver value in order to influence target audience behaviors [sic] that benefit society (public health, safety, the environment, and communities) as well as the target audience'.

*Change4Life* forms part of Public Health England's (PHE) 'Starting Well' brand architecture, which also incorporates *Start4Life*, *Talk to Frank* and *Rise Above*. PHE say that the 'Starting Well' campaigns aim to support their priorities of reducing childhood obesity and ensuring children have the best start in life, whilst campaigns that fall under their *Living Well* and *Ageing Well* umbrellas focus on preventative health campaigns for adults, recognition of common conditions and raising the importance of early treatment (PHE, 2017). If you are familiar with *Change4Life*, which is aimed at supporting families with children aged between 3 and 11, you might also have heard of *Start4Life*, which focuses on supporting pregnant women and their babies and young children.

The behaviours *Change4Life* are seeking to modify are in regard to healthy practices in:

- Reducing sugar intake ('Sugar Swaps')
- Increasing consumption of fruit and vegetables ('5 A Day')

- Having structured meals, especially breakfast ('Meal Time')
- Reducing unhealthy snacking ('Snack Check')
- Reducing portion size ('Me Size Meals')
- Reducing fat consumption ('Cut Back Fat')
- 60 minutes of moderate intensity activity ('60 Active Minutes')
- Reducing sedentary behaviour ('Up & About')

(National Social Marketing Centre, 2011)

Early research conducted on the campaign has found that it was effective in drawing awareness to the initiative, although evidence that *Change4Life* has actually changed healthy practices is limited. A year after the campaign was launched, an early evaluation found that 99% of mothers with a child aged under 11 had had an opportunity to see the advertising campaign, and more than one million mothers said that they had made changes to how their children ate and what physical activity they did (Department of Health, 2010). Yet it is important to note that this is what mothers *claimed* to the researchers, but it does not necessarily mean that changes to children's diet and activity levels have been *observed*. More recent research suggests that since the campaign has been running, the percentage of children doing the recommended amount of daily physical activity has decreased, while the percentage of children classed as obese has stayed the same (Chalkley and Milton, 2021). This suggests that whilst the campaign is intended to improve children's physical health practices by capitalising on their, and their parents', media usage, evidence is limited that it has had an impact on their diet and physical activity levels.

## Advertisements for unhealthy foods

Whilst children may be seeing *Change4Life* advertisements on television promoting healthy habits such as reducing sugar intake and being aware of the 'traffic light' system on food products, they may also be viewing advertisements for unhealthy food items. In February 2020 the World Health Organization recommended the need to 'tighten national regulation of harmful commercial marketing', as they claim exposure to unhealthy food and drinks advertising is contributing to rising levels of obesity in children. This is something that the UK's Department of Health and Social Care agrees with, and it has thus stipulated that new restrictions on advertising for foods high in fat, salt and sugar (HFSS) are to come into force in 2022. Advertisements for HFSS food products will only be able to be aired on television and on-demand services after a 9pm watershed and before 5:30am, and paid-for online advertisements will also only be shown between these times (Department of Health and Social Care, 2021).

In order to decide what restrictions should be put in place, a consultation took place to gather views from the wider public (Department for Digital, Culture, Media and Sport and Department of Health and Social Care, 2021): 1,736 individuals replied, who were a mixture of professionals from organisations such as charities, government, the NHS, social care and the private sector. A small proportion of respondents were parents, who wanted to share their views on what the restrictions on HFSS food advertising should be. Most of the respondents were in favour of a watershed for advertising HFSS products on television and online. In addition, the government examined research from a variety of sources, for instance on the impact of screen advertising on children's diet and also about advertising on HFSS foods. One of the studies examined found that 'short-term exposure to unhealthy food advertising on TV and advergames increases immediate calorie consumption in children' (Russell, Croker and Viner, 2019, p. 554), thus stressing the importance of limiting how many advertisements for unhealthy products children see.

You might not have come across the term 'advergames' before. The Advertising Standards Authority (2012) describes them as 'electronic games that are used to advertise a product, brand or an organisation. They are accessible on social media sites, companies' own websites and as downloadable content or apps on mobile devices.' Another of the pieces of research the Department of Health and Social Care explored before implementing the new restrictions was conducted by Cancer Research UK. Ng, Froguel and Clark (2020), on behalf of Cancer Research UK, analysed advertisements broadcast on television in the UK in September 2019. They found that almost 50% of the food advertisements broadcast on ITV1, Channel 4, Channel 5 and Sky One during that month were for HFSS products, and between 6pm and 9pm this rose to 55% of food advertisements. The most common advertisements were for delivery brands, as well as for foods such as chocolate, sweets, cakes and biscuits. In contrast, only 6% of food advertisements shown between 6pm and 9pm were for fruit and vegetables.

### Time to consider

Imagine you are responsible for an element of the *Change4Life* social marketing campaign. How would you design an advert to promote healthy eating and physical activity? You might want to think about:

- Who your target audience is
- What message you want to get across
- What the purpose of the advert would be
- Where you would want your advert to be shown or broadcast
- How you would evaluate whether your advert had been successful

## The impact of social media on children's mental health

Back in Chapter 2 (*Children's media lives*) we considered some statistics about young children's media use. For instance, 4% of 5–7 year olds have a social media profile (Ofcom, 2020). This rises to 21% of 8–11 year olds and 71% of 12–15 year olds. These figures are rising year on year, which means that considering the impact of children's social media engagement is of increasing importance. Several reports have been written that consider the links between children's social media presence and their mental health, including those by Frith (2017) and the Royal Society for Public Health (RSPH) (2017). The reports are slightly different in style; whereas Frith is sharing evidence that has come from a range of UK and international studies focusing on children's mental health and their social media use, the RSPH conducted their own primary research about users' views of five of the most popular social media platforms: Facebook, Instagram, Snapchat, Twitter and YouTube. Now, what we need to bear in mind with both of these reports is that they are predominantly focusing on statistics and research conducted with teenagers and young people; in fact participants in the RSPH's (2017) study were aged between 14 and 24 years old. You may think 'well, these aren't young children', and of course you would be right. But it is important to consider that the young children in early years settings today, that you may be studying or working with, are growing up in a world heavily influenced by social media. In fact, many of the children in early years settings today will be coming into contact with 16–24 year olds as their parents, siblings or ECEC practitioners, and thus will be indirectly influenced by the impact that social media is having on those people's lives.

Frith's (2017) report is *Social Media and Children's Mental Health: A Review of the Evidence*. It looks at existing evidence into the relationship between young people's wellbeing and social media usage, examining the positive impacts, the online risks and harm to children and young people and how they respond to those risks. She states that some of the positive implications of social media can be connecting with family and friends, making new friendships, developing an identity, community involvement, collaborating on projects (such as through a homework WhatsApp group) and accessing health information online. She cites the Organisation for Economic Cooperation and Development (OECD) (2015) who, in a study of 15 year olds' wellbeing, found that over 90% of both boys and girls in the UK agreed or strongly agreed that it is useful to have social networks online, higher than the average in the 35 OECD countries as a whole (OECD, 2015).

However, Frith also shares concerns about the risks and potential harms of social media for mental health and wellbeing. These include spending excessive time online, which teenagers say can impact on their sleep and schoolwork, oversharing of information, including personal information and nude images, cyberbullying, lower body esteem and accessing harmful information and advice online. Frith (2017) cites the Office for National Statistics (2015) who have found a positive correlation between how much time is spent on social media and mental health problems. High social media use has been linked with social isolation, anxieties about conforming to social norms, decreased attention, hyperactivity, aggression and anti-social behaviour (Frith, 2017). The RSPH (2017) report shares similar concerns about the potential positive and negative effects of social media. As well as repeating concerns about the impact on mental health conditions like anxiety and depression, sleep, body image and cyberbullying, their participants also spoke about FOMO (fear of missing out). The RSPH (2017, p. 12) describes this as 'the worry that social events, or otherwise enjoyable activities, may be taking place without you present to enjoy them', as users browse photos and content about other people's lives that means they question what they are missing out on in their own. This can lead to feelings of anxiety and inadequacy, though not in all cases.

## Time to consider

Have a closer look at Frith's (2017) report. It is a very useful and accessible report that shares findings from a wide range of studies, both from the UK and internationally, about the links between social media and children's mental health and wellbeing, both in terms of what the positive effects can be as well as the negative impacts. Here's the reference:

Frith, E. (2017) *Social Media and Children's Mental Health: A Review of the Evidence*. Available at: https://epi.org.uk/wp-content/uploads/2017/06/Social-Media_Mental-Health_EPI-Report.pdf (accessed 11 March 2020).

Have a think about the answers to these questions:

- Have a look at the list of positive impacts of social media on page 15. Rank these in order of their importance. How can you make links to these points and children's health?
- Page 17 lists five risks of social media on children's mental health and wellbeing. Read through the explanation of each of these, and decide which risk is most pressing. Why?
- Considering all of the risks listed, what steps can be taken to minimise these? How might the government take measures to minimise these risks?

## Messenger Kids

Although the social media platforms considered by Frith and the RSPH are aimed at those older than young children, these platforms are diversifying to increase awareness of their sites and capture children's brand loyalty before they are old enough to officially open their own accounts. One such attempt is *Messenger Kids*, an app created by Facebook marketed as a way for children aged under 13 to instant message and video chat with their friends and family (Facebook, 2017). Facebook claim that the app is a safe way for children to engage in online communication which is ad-free and has far-reaching parental controls, in response to demand from parents for such a product. Yet in 2018, the Campaign for a Commercial-Free Childhood wrote an open letter to Mark Zuckerberg, founder of *Facebook*, in response to *Messenger Kids*, urging him to discontinue the app.

The letter states, 'a growing body of research demonstrates that excessive use of digital devices and social media is harmful to children and teens, making it very likely this new app will undermine children's healthy development'. The letter called for the app to be discontinued, stating:

> Younger children are simply not ready to have social media accounts. They are not old enough to navigate the complexities of online relationships, which often lead to misunderstandings and conflicts even among more mature users. They also do not have a fully developed understanding of privacy, including what's appropriate to share with others and who has access to their conversations, pictures, and videos.

The letter continues that *Messenger Kids* is likely to increase the amount of time children spend on social media, exacerbating the problem of parents regulating their children's screen time and making it harder for children to foster face-to-face relationships, which are important to learn how to read emotions and body language. The letter's authors claim that rather than **responding** to a need for children to have a safe online platform to digitally communicate with friends and family, it is instead **creating** that need, and otherwise children who did not have their own social media accounts could use their parents' accounts or simply call. They suggest that those children and teens who already have social media accounts such as with Snapchat and Instagram are unlikely to be converted to using a child-specific Facebook one instead.

Despite the letter, *Messenger Kids* continues to exist and, in March 2021, plans were announced to create an Instagram app for those aged under 13. Again, the Campaign for a Commercial-Free Childhood appealed to Mark Zuckerberg (as Facebook owns Instagram) to not launch a children's version of Instagram, citing the dangers of social media for children's mental health and wellbeing, amongst other things (Campaign for a Commercial-Free Childhood, 2021). At the time of writing, no 'Instagram for children' app had been launched, although Facebook told BBC News in 2021 that children are already online, so the app will support them to do that in a safe and age-appropriate way (Wakefield, 2021).

## Time to consider

On the one hand, Facebook claim that apps such as *Messenger Kids* and a children's version of Instagram ensure that under 13s, who they argue are already online, are communicating with their friends and family online, and sharing images online, in a safe and controlled way. On the other, the Campaign for a Commercial-Free Childhood suggests that the apps will encourage children to increase their social media usage, with negative implications. What do you think? Complete Table 5.1 to help you think about what the pros and cons of such apps might be.

**TABLE 5.1** Pros and cons of child-specific social media apps

| Pros of child-specific social media apps | Cons of child-specific social media apps |
| --- | --- |
| *E.g. They may have extra safety measures in place.* | *E.g. They may encourage children to spend more time online than previously.* |

## Final reflection

In this chapter we have considered the relationship between media usage and children's health. We have looked at what the link may be between children's media use and physical health, and how campaigns such as *Change4Life* attempt to use social marketing to encourage families to adopt healthier lifestyle practices with regard to diet and healthy eating. We have also explored the link between media use, specifically social media use, and children and young people's mental health. Excessive social media use may exacerbate anxiety and depression, sleep problems, FOMO (fear of missing out), body image and cyberbullying. However, social media use can also be a platform to form and maintain relationships, build online communities, allow a forum for self-expression and self-identity and access health information. Whilst there are certainly negative implications of media use on children's physical and mental health, parents and practitioners need to consider how these can be minimised so that children are in a position to take advantage of the benefits that media usage can have on their health. If we are to believe executives at Facebook, children and young people are online anyway, and thus need to be supported to do so safely and with appropriate controls. This is something that later chapters will consider.

## Key points

- Media usage may have a detrimental impact on a child's physical health, in particular regarding their weight, diet, physical activity levels and sleep habits. Strategies like *Change4Life* have increased awareness of what healthy practices for children are, but there is limited evidence that the initiative has been effective in changing children's diet and activity levels.
- Media usage, in particular social media platforms, can be detrimental to a child's mental health. It may exacerbate conditions such as anxiety and depression, lead to FOMO (fear of missing out) and increase opportunities for bullying. However, such platforms do also create outlets for self-expression and identity and can be a useful source of health advice for young people.

## Further reading

1. Royal Society for Public Health (2017) *#StatusofMind*. Available at: www.rsph.org.uk/static/uploaded/d125b27c-0b62-41c5-a2c0155a8887cd01.pdf (accessed 30 August 2021).Although this focuses on the links between the mental health of young people (aged between 16 and 24) and social media, it is still definitely worth a read. We can speculate that there would be similar outcomes, both positive and negative, for children aged under 16 too, and certainly the RSPH's 'calls to action' are applicable to all ages across the board.
2. Canadian Paediatric Society, Digital Health Task Force, Ottawa, Ontario (2017) 'Screen Time and Young Children: Promoting Health and Development in a Digital World', *Paediatrics & Child Health*, 22(8), pp. 461–468. DOI: https://doi.org/10.1093/pch/pxx123.Unlike the first further reading, this one focuses specifically on young children. It is a literature search about the impact of screen media on children aged under 5 and breaks down the effects into three types of impact: developmental, psychosocial and physical. For each of these three types, the potential benefits and risks of screen time are considered, followed by guidelines for best practice for parents and practitioners.

## References


Adachi, P.J.C. and Willoughby, T. (2017) 'The Link Between Playing Video Games and Positive Youth Outcomes', *Child Development Perspectives*, 11(3), pp. 202–206.

Advertising Standards Authority (2012) *Advergames*. Available at: www.asa.org.uk/news/advergames.html (accessed 30 August 2021).

American Academy of Pediatrics (2016) 'Media and Young Minds: Council on Communications and Media', *Pediatrics*, 135(4): e20162591. DOI: 10.1542/peds.2016-2591.

Baranowski, T., Abdelsamad, D., Baranowski, J., O'Connor, T.M., Thompson, D., Barnett, A., Cerin, E. and Chen, T. (2012) 'Impact of an Active Video Game on Healthy Children's Physical Activity', *Pediatrics*, 129(3): e636-642. DOI: 10.1542/peds.2011-2050.

Campaign for a Commercial-Free Childhood (2018) *Re: Facebook Messenger Kids*. Available at: https://fairplayforkids.org/wp-content/uploads/archive/devel generate/gaw/FB MessengerKids.pdf (accessed 30 August 2021).

Campaign for a Commercial-Free Childhood (2021) *Instagram Letter*. Available at: https://fairplayforkids.org/wp-content/uploads/2021/04/instagram_letter.pdf (accessed 30 August 2021).

Chalkley, A. and Milton, K. (2021) 'A Critical Review of National Physical Activity Policies Relating to Children and Young People in England', *Journal of Sport and Health Science*, 10(3), pp. 255–262.

Coleman, R. (2016) 'Calculating Obesity, Pre-emptive Power and the Politics of Futurity: The Case of *Change4Life*', in L. Amoore and V. Piotukh (eds), *Algorithmic Life: Calculative Devices in the Age of Big Data*. London: Routledge, pp. 176–190.

Cox, R., Skouteris, H., Rutherford, L., Fuller-Tyskiewicz, M., Dell'Aquila, D. and Hardy, L.L. (2013) 'Television Viewing, Television Content, Food Intake, Physical Activity and Body Mass Index: A Cross-Sectional Study of Preschool Children Aged 2–6 Years', *Health Promotion Journal of Australia*, 23(1), pp. 58–62.

Department for Digital, Culture, Media and Sport and Department of Health and Social Care (2021) *Introducing further advertising restrictions on TV and online for products high in fat, salt and sugar: government response*. Available at: www.gov.uk/government/consultations/further-advertising-restrictions-for-products-high-in-fat-salt-and-sugar/outcome/introducing-further-advertising-restrictions-on-tv-and-online-for-products-high-in-fat-salt-and-sugar-government-response (accessed 30 August 2021).

Department of Health (2010) *Change4Life One Year On*. Available at: https://webarchive.nationalarchives.gov.uk/20130124053508/http://www.dh.gov.uk/prod_consum_dh/groups/dh_digitalassets/@dh/@en/documents/digitalasset/dh_115511.pdf (accessed 30 August 2021).

Department of Health and Social Care (2021) *New advertising rules to help tackle childhood obesity*. Available at: www.gov.uk/government/news/new-advertising-rules-to-help-tackle-childhood-obesity (accessed 30 August 2021).

Facebook (2017) *Introducing Messenger Kids, a New App for Families to Connect*. Available at: https://about.fb.com/news/2017/12/introducing-messenger-kids-a-new-app-for-families-to-connect/ (accessed 30 August 2021).

Fisher, P.G. (2019) 'To Sleep and Dream without Digital Screens', *The Journal of Pediatrics*, 205, p. 2.

Frith, E. (2017) *Social Media and Children's Mental Health: A Review of the Evidence*. Available at: https://epi.org.uk/wp-content/uploads/2017/06/Social-Media_Mental-Health_EPI-Report.pdf (accessed 30 August 2021).

Garrison, M.M., Liekweg, K. and Christakis, D.A. (2011) 'Media Use and Child Sleep: The Impact of Content, Timing, and Environment', *Pediatrics*, 128(1), pp. 29–35.

Hale, L., Kirschen, G.W., LeBourgeois, M.K., Gradisar, M., Garrison, M.M., Montgomery-Downs, H., Kirschen, H., McHale, S.M., Chang, A. and Buxton, O.M. (2018) 'Youth Screen Media Habits and Sleep: Sleep-Friendly Screen-Behavior Recommendations for Clinicians, Educators, and Parents', *Child and Adolescent Psychiatric Clinics of North America*, 27(2), pp. 229–245.

Kirsh, S.J. (2010) *Media and Youth: A Developmental Perspective*. Chichester: Wiley-Blackwell.

Kotler, P. and Lee, N.R. (2008) *Social Marketing – Influencing Behaviors for Good*. Thousand Oaks, CA: Sage.

LeBlanc, A.G., Chaput, J., McFarlane, A., Colley, R.C., Thivel, D., Biddle, S.J.H., Maddison, R., Leatherdale, S.T. and Tremblay, M.S. (2013) 'Active Video Games and Health Indicators in Children and Youth: A Systematic Review', *Plos One*, DOI: https://doi.org/10.1371/journal.pone.0065351.

Lindon, J. (2011) *Too Safe for Their Own Good?* London: NCB.

Lindqvist, A., Castelli, D., Hallberg, J. and Rutberg, S. (2018) 'The Praise and Price of Pokémon GO: A Qualitative Study of Children's and Parents' Experiences', *JMIR Serious Games*, 6(1): e1. DOI: 10.2196/games.8979

Ng, D., Froguel, A. and Clark, M. (2020) *Analysis of revenue for ITV1, Channel 4, Channel 5 and Sky One derived from HFSS TV advertising spots in September 2019*. Available at: www.cancerresearchuk.org/sites/default/files/cruk_report_on_sept19_nielsen_tv_ad_analysis_-_final22july20.pdf (accessed 30 August 2021).

NHS (2020) *Change4Life*. Available at: www.nhs.uk/change4life (accessed 30 August 2021).

Ofcom (2020) *Children and Parents: Media Use and Attitudes Report 2019*. Available at: www.ofcom.org.uk/__data/assets/pdf_file/0023/190616/children-media-use-attitudes-2019-report.pdf (accessed 30 August 2021).

Organisation for Economic Cooperation and Development (2015) *PISA 2015 Results: Students' Well-being, Volume 3*. Available at: https://read.oecd-ilibrary.org/education/pisa-2015-results-volume-iii_9789264273856-en#page1 (accessed 30 August 2021).

Peng, W., Lin, J. and Crouse, J. (2011) 'Is Playing Exergames Really Exercising? A Meta-Analysis of Energy Expenditure in Active Video Games', *Cyberpsychology, Behavior, and Social Networking*, 14(11), pp. 681–688. DOI: 10.1089/cyber.2010.0578.

Przybylski, A.K. (2019) 'Digital Screen Time and Pediatric Sleep: Evidence from a Preregistered Cohort Study', *The Journal of Pediatrics*, 205, pp. 218–223.

Public Health England (2017) *Social Marketing Strategy 2017 to 2020*. Available at: https://assets.publishing.service.gov.uk/government/uploads/system/uploads/attachment_data/file/646715/public_health_england_marketing_strategy_2017_to_2020.pdf (accessed 30 August 2021).

Royal Society for Public Health (2017) *#StatusofMind*. Available at: www.rsph.org.uk/static/uploaded/d125b27c-0b62-41c5-a2c0155a8887cd01.pdf (accessed 30 August 2021).

Russell, S.J., Croker, H. and Viner, R.M. (2019) 'The Effect of Screen Advertising on Children's Dietary Intake: A Systematic Review and Meta-Analysis', *Obesity Reviews*, 20(4), pp. 554–568.

Wakefield, J. (2021) *Facebook urged to scrap Instagram for children plans*. Available at: www.bbc.co.uk/news/technology-56757586 (accessed 30 August 2021).

World Health Organization (2020) *World failing to provide children with a healthy life and a climate fit for their future: WHO-UNICEF-Lancet*. Available at: www.who.int/news-room/detail/19-02-2020-world-failing-to-provide-children-with-a-healthy-life-and-a-climate-fit-for-their-future-who-unicef-lancet (accessed 30 August 2021).

PART

# II

# How does the media construct childhood?

CHAPTER

6

# Children as consumers

## The impact of advertising

What's the last advert you remember watching, reading or listening to? Chances are, you might not even remember, but it still might have an influence on your purchasing decisions next time you shop. Now think back to when you were a child – how did you react to seeing adverts? And what do you think the risks might be of children viewing them? This chapter will begin by examining the four risks of screen media, including the commercial risks of advertising (Blum-Ross and Livingstone, 2016) and the impact of a commercialised childhood (Guldberg, 2009). We will then look at the Bailey Review (2011) into the commercialisation and sexualisation of children's lives and how the government has responded to the recommendations Bailey made. Finally, we will consider what parents and children identify are the adverts that bother them (ASA, 2012), and then examine the role of charity adverts in the construction of the modern child (O'Dell, 2008).

So far in this book, we have mainly been thinking about how media sources that children are actively choosing to engage with – such as television programmes, video games and websites – have an impact on children. We have thought briefly in Chapter 5 (*Media and children's health*) about the role that adverts can play in children's development, particularly their physical development, such as adverts for campaigns like *Change4Life* or for unhealthy foods. But now we are moving on to think about the other ways that the media has an impact on children. In this chapter we are going to think in more detail about the impact of advertising on young children. We will be thinking about how this may be contributing to the commercialisation of childhood and also the way in which children are viewed as a result of their portrayal in charity advertisements.

## Commercial risks of screen media

When you think about the risks of children's media usage, what do you think of? For many people, the commercial risks may not be the ones that immediately

DOI: 10.4324/9781003121206-8

spring to mind. Traditionally, the risks of screen media use have been described as the three 'C's – conduct risks, content risks and contact risks (Millwood Hargrave and Livingstone, 2009). Yet Blum-Ross and Livingstone (2016, p. 9) add a fourth C to their list of risks associated with screen media, which is *commercial* risks. They describe the four types as follows:

- Conduct risks e.g. bullying, 'sexting' or misuse of personal information.
- Content risks e.g. pornographic, violent, racist, false or misleading content.
- Contact risks e.g. 'stranger danger', stalking, harassment or impersonation.
- Commercial risks e.g. advertising, excessive or hidden marketing, in-app purchases or scams.

(Blum-Ross and Livingstone, 2016, p. 9)

It is this final 'C' that we are considering in this chapter. Let's take a moment to think about the way in which Blum-Ross and Livingstone (2016) describe commercial risks. The first – advertising – is probably the most obvious. Children come across advertising frequently on screen media, whether it is whilst watching television or YouTube, or whilst browsing websites, engaging with apps or playing online games. The second – excessive or hidden marketing – is a little trickier to grasp, but it is the notion that children may be subject to disproportionate levels of marketing, which are not clearly acknowledged as such. We thought about advergames in Chapter 5 (*Media and children's health*) and they are a good example of a type of marketing that is hidden. Sponsorship and product placement may also fall into this category. The third – in-app purchases – is of growing concern. A survey by Childnet International (2015) found that 12% of children aged between 11 and 18 had accidentally spent money on an in-app purchase, often because they didn't realise that it cost money, or that it cost real money. The fourth – scams – is a risk particularly affecting younger people. A myriad of financial scams became prominent as a result of Covid-19, such as fake texts or emails purporting to be from services such as NHS Track and Trace, the Royal Mail and TV Licensing. Younger people were more likely to pay out money than older people: only 1% of over 55s stated they had paid out money to such scams, in comparison to 16% of 18–24 year olds (Financial Conduct Authority, 2021). This perhaps suggests that young children need more support and information to help them recognise scams, so that they do not become part of the 16% when they reach 18.

Millwood Hargrave and Livingstone (2009) have suggested that the commercial risks of screen media is an area where research is lacking. They do, however, cite a now dated study conducted by Fielder et al. (2007) that found that whilst adults are more *au fait* with the risks of the other big 'C's, parents do not prioritise the risks of commercial content when considering their children's online safety. As a result, some children find advertisements online hard to recognise, particularly if marketers employ the advergaming techniques we considered in Chapter 5 (*Media and children's health*). Nairn and Dew (2007) note how advergames are not always labelled as adverts and recommend that children 'need to be told quite clearly when the words, pictures, sounds and images that appear on their screen are attempting to persuade them, sell to them or create an impression for commercial ends' (p. 43). This is something that has, to some extent, been taken on board since Nairn and Dew's 2007 recommendation. Plus, social media influencers are now required as part of the Advertising Code to ensure that any content they are paid to create to advertise a product or as part of a commercial partnership is clearly labelled as such. There is also specific guidance for online advertisements aimed at under 12s, which may be part of an online game, branded online video content or via an influencer (Committee of Advertising Practice, 2021). Advertisements in these cases must be (a) 'prominent' (i.e. so it is clearly displayed the content is an advert), (b) 'interruptive' (i.e. so it is 'readily apparent' (p. 4) to the child), and (c) 'sufficient to identify the marketer and the commercial intent' (i.e. so a child can tell who is advertising it and that they are doing so).

### Time to consider

Think about the advertisements that you encounter, whether they are on television, pop-ups on websites, paid-for promotions by influencers or on the radio. How do you think it could be made clearer to children that these are advertisements, with the purpose of persuading them to make, or to influence, a purchase?

## The 'commercialisation of childhood'

The commitment to making children more aware of when they are encountering advertisements fits with the concern around the 'commercialisation of childhood'. As the disposable income of families has grown, so too has the amount of advertising that is targeted to them, especially to children who may use 'pester power' to persuade parents to buy toys and games on their behalf. This is something raised by Linn (2004, cited in Guldberg, 2009, p. 113), who suggests children's 'health, education, creativity, and values – are at risk of being compromised by their status in the market place'. Before we go any further, can you think about the ways in which seeing children as consumers who have a 'status in the market place' may be detrimental to children's health, education, creativity and values, as Linn suggests?

Essentially what Linn is saying is that media advertising is having an impact on many aspects of a child's life. It also, Guldberg suggests, feeds a 'snobbish contempt for "ignorant" "materialistic" children and "weak" and "inept" parents' (2009, p. 116) who seemingly cannot say no to their children's demands and pester power for the items they have seen advertised. Buckingham (2005) agrees that this is the dominant view of the child in relation to media, i.e. 'the incompetent child – the child that is too immature, too irrational, too inexperienced, too cognitively undeveloped, to know what is happening or to be able to resist it' (2005, p. 6). Yet he juxtaposes this with the view of the 'media competent child', who, he suggests, is often much more knowledgeable than we might think about advertising, and able to recognise and critique the outlandish claims often made in adverts. Thus, when thinking about how children are constructed in relation to media advertising, we have got competing notions of the child as ignorant and materialistic, and of the child as competent and critical. Which perspective best fits with how you view children in relation to advertising? We will come back to the idea of the construction of children and childhoods later in this chapter.

## The Bailey Review

One of the dangers of the commercialisation of childhood is that it may lead to the sexualisation of childhood. In 2011, Bailey was commissioned by the government to write a report about the commercialisation and sexualisation of children, entitled *Letting Children Be Children*. Four key themes emerged: the culture children are growing up in is becoming increasingly sexualised, with limited regulation; clothing and services for children are also increasingly sexualised and gender-stereotyped; children are being pressured to become consumers, which brings benefits but risks too; parents don't feel they have a voice in challenging the sexualisation or commercialisation of their children's childhoods. The report gave 14 recommendations to regulators and government on how to 'let children be children' moving forward. For instance, the third recommendation proposed 'ensuring the content of pre-watershed television programming better meets parents' expectations' (Bailey, 2011, p. 15), whilst Recommendation 7 suggested 'Ensuring that the regulation of advertising reflects more closely parents' and children's views' (p. 17).

A strength of Bailey's report is how he believes that the commercialisation and sexualisation of childhood should be countered. He states that contributors to the review tended to advocate one of two opposing approaches that could be taken. First, that children should be kept 'wholly innocent and unknowing until they are adults' because 'the world is a nasty place and children should be unsullied by it until they are mature enough to deal with it' (2011, p. 10). This approach adopts the belief that 'children can be easily led astray, so that even glimpses of the adult world will hurry them into adulthood' (ibid.). This fits with the perspective of the child as vulnerable, which is something we will come back to in Chapter 7 (*Innocent, invisible or feral: Constructions of children in the media*). It also fits with the traditional view of the child (Jones, 2009), something we'll return to later on in this chapter.

The second approach that contributors expressed in the review was that we should accept the status quo: 'we should accept the world for what it is and simply give children the tools to understand it and navigate their way through it better' (Bailey, 2011, p. 10). This viewpoint fits with the emerging view of the child (Jones, 2009) as powerful, capable and confident, and not as 'passive receivers … or simple imitators of adults; rather they willingly interact with the commercial and sexualised world and consume what it has to offer' (Bailey, 2011, p. 10). The viewpoint suggests that if we make attempts to keep children innocent this will lead to adults also being treated as children, so instead we should treat children as adults. The two approaches align with the two views of the child in relation to media that Buckingham (2005) discusses. He suggests: 'On the one hand, we have a construction of the incompetent child, the child as vulnerable innocent, as media victim; and on the other, we have the celebration of the competent child, the child as sophisticated, media literate, autonomous' (Buckingham, 2005, pp. 10–11).

In Chapter 7 (*Innocent, invisible or feral: Constructions of children in the media*) we will consider that newspapers often support the narrative of the incompetent, vulnerable, innocent child, which is often seen in advertisements too. Australian research identified that children are portrayed as '"precious", "pure", "uncivilised" and "vulnerable"' (Lupton, 2014, p. 341), for instance the 'precious' image of parents cuddling their newborns in adverts for nappies, or the 'pure' image of a contented sleeping infant on a carpet, intended to 'seek to transfer the meanings of the sleeping baby – innocence, purity, softness – to the carpet' (p. 344). Yet despite how they are portrayed in adverts, Buckingham (2005) argues that the advertising industry itself promotes the discourse that children are instead competent and media savvy. Can you think why this may be? Of course, if children are media literate, it is not necessary to impose tighter regulations on advertising to children, something that obviously the advertising industry is opposed to.

Bailey himself argues that to be effective in combating the commercialisation and sexualisation of childhood a mixture of the two approaches is needed. To some extent children do need shielding from some of the commercialisation and sexualisation of the modern world. However, on the other hand, instilling them with age-appropriate knowledge and information to help them understand and critique the world they are a part of is vital. The strength of this approach, Bailey suggests, is at the same time that society makes a conscious effort not to further the commercialisation and sexualisation of childhood, children are also given the skills to navigate the twenty-first-century world they are a part of. Buckingham (2005) may suggest that a focus on media literacy is a cop-out on the part of those in power: 'since the government is not going to exercise control, people will have to do it for themselves' (2005, p. 8). But Bailey stresses that children need the help of adults to teach them. Parents have a role to play here, as do regulators and those working in media and industry.

The government responded to Bailey's set of recommendations in 2013 and set out what progress had been made in the 18 months since his report was published (Department for Education (DfE), 2013). For instance, in response to Recommendation 3, that content of pre-watershed programming better meets parents' expectations, they say that in September 2011, Ofcom published new guidance to help broadcasters make the transition from pre- to post-watershed. The DfE's report also stated that Ofcom had increased how much parents were consulted about their concerns on pre-watershed programming, something we considered in Chapter 4 (*Viewing violence: Just a moral panic?*) when we thought about both parents' and non-parents' views about violent content on television.

In Recommendation 7, Bailey had recommended 'ensuring that the regulation of advertising reflects more closely parents' and children's views', adding that the Advertising Standards Authority (ASA) should conduct research with families about how the ASA regulates adverts. The DfE report that, in response to this, the ASA published a report about harm and offence in advertising in 2012, which we will go on to talk about in more detail later.

## Time to consider

Let's come back to the two approaches that Bailey (2011) shares:

1. The world is an overly commercialised and sexualised place. Children should be shielded from it for as long as possible to protect their innocence.
2. The world is an overly commercialised and sexualised place and children need to learn to live with this. They have the capabilities to do so.

And then remember the two opposing constructions of children that Buckingham (2005, pp. 10–11) reports:

1. The incompetent child, the child as vulnerable innocent, as media victim.
2. The competent child, the child as sophisticated, media literate, autonomous.

Look at these two sets of statements. Which ones do you agree with? Why? Can you see any links between them? And can you see any strengths in Bailey's suggestion to take elements of both approaches when considering how to tackle the issue of the commercialisation and sexualisation of childhood?

## What do children say about advertising?

As we said earlier, one of the results of Bailey's report was that the Advertising Standards Agency conducted research in 2012 to explore what bothered the general public, both adults and children, in relation to adverts. As part of the research, 1,020 children aged between 11 and 16 completed an online survey about adverts. In addition, group interviews with six peer friendship groups and four family groups took place. The ASA stated that many children were initially unwilling to share that there were adverts that bothered them; perhaps this was because they could not identify adverts that concerned them, or perhaps because they felt peer pressure or vulnerability in admitting they had apprehensions about some adverts. However, some children stated that there were adverts that had bothered them, and others instead talked of adverts that they thought would bother other children. Before you read on, can you think of what adverts these might be?

The child participants in the ASA's study mentioned that the advertisements that bothered them included those that were violent or scary, those that had sexual content, those that portrayed an idealised body image, and those for public service (i.e. for a road safety campaign). Can you think of any adverts you've seen recently that fall into these categories? There were some differences in which adverts boys and girls expressed concerns about; girls were more likely to talk about the portrayal of body image than boys, whilst some boys disclosed that they felt uncomfortable about an anti-rape campaign advert and 'while they had understood the broad intention of the advert, they were not completely clear on its purpose and were likely to ask peers for clarification' (ASA, 2012, p. 37). Spontaneously, some children also stated they had been bothered by charity adverts. Can you think of why this might be? The ASA identify two reasons. Some children were bothered by the causes of the adverts themselves, which were for charities supporting causes such as cancer research, international aid and animal welfare. Other children were concerned that they weren't in a position to help the charities, for instance saying 'we can't sponsor. We can't give money to them, they're asking for us to give but we're too young' (ASA, 2012, p. 37).

The research also explored adults' views about harm and offence in advertising. The study found that both parents and non-parents were conscious that the media, including advertising, might be harmful to children in relation to many of the same themes that children identified, including charity adverts, body image, sexual content and nudity, and the commercialisation of childhood. In relation to this last theme, adults expressed concerns about how children were exposed to adverts, and how 'parents felt the intention was to make them feel guilty and their children disappointed if they did not get what they wanted' (p. 36). This fits with the notion of 'pester power', which is something discussed in the Bailey Review (2011). Bailey reports that 32% of children acknowledge that if they want something and their parents won't buy it for them, they'll keep asking until they get it. Maybe you wouldn't want to admit this, but were you a child like that? 20% of children also acknowledged that liking the adverts is a factor in wanting to buy a particular toy, gadget or item of clothing (Bailey, 2011, p. 58).

### Time to consider

Imagine you are a participant in the ASA's (2012) research. If you were asked to talk about adverts that might bother children, what would you say? Now imagine you are the researcher: what questions would you ask adults, and then children, to find out information about what concerns them about television advertising?

## How are children portrayed in adverts?

So far in this book we've thought about the different ways that the media can have an impact on children, whether that be on their academic attainment, their behaviour, their emotional state, their physical health or their mental health. We've been thinking about how it has an impact due to children's **usage**, i.e. children engaging with types of media sources has an effect on how they learn, develop and grow. But now in this chapter we are going to begin to think about how the media has an impact on children and childhoods whether they engage with media sources or not. This is because of how media sources **construct** childhoods. This is something we will continue to think about in Chapter 7 (*Innocent, invisible or feral: Constructions of children in the media*).

We have looked at what children make of charity adverts, but what is also interesting is how charity adverts portray children. Take a moment to think about how the way in which children are shown in the media, for instance how they behave, act or look, might have an effect on how people treat them. Now take a moment to think about what the purpose of a charity advert is. On the whole, it is to encourage the viewer or reader to make a monetary donation to that particular charity. That means that those responsible for the advertisement campaign need to consider how children are shown, and what images and behaviours are shown.

## Time to consider

Take a moment to recall any television advertisements you may have seen featuring children. If you can't think of any, look online for adverts for charities such as Save the Children, Barnardo's or the NSPCC. What are children doing in those adverts? How do the adverts make you feel?

Some of the children's charity adverts you have seen might be for charities which support children who have been victims of abuse. We need to consider how victims of child abuse are portrayed in the media, because that influences how we define who is at risk, what we mean by 'risk' and what stereotypical portrayals of children might be. To do this, we are going to specifically consider an advertising campaign by the children's charity Barnardo's, which took place between 1999 and 2003. It aimed to make connections between 'childhood disadvantage and the practical, physical and emotional consequences experienced in adulthood', and was aimed at 35–55-year-old individuals: 'affluent potential donors who might still associate Barnardo's with an older image of charity orphanages rather than the desired image of a modern professional child protection organisation' (Nunn, 2004, p. 280). These adverts have been analysed in a piece of research conducted by O'Dell in 2008. O'Dell (2008) states:

> The advertisements were produced for Barnardo's in three phases. In the first set of adverts a situation of danger was depicted, such as a street with a car stopped to pick up a prostitute or an alley with signs of drug use. A child's image is overlaid on the site of danger so that it shows the child engaging in a dangerous (adult) activity. In the second set of advertisements an adult in danger or dead was depicted alongside text about the adult as a child. The final phase of the advertisement campaigns depicted a child whose image had been altered so that their face and hair looked very old. Thus in each of the series of advertisements the images and texts juxtapose adults with their child selves and fracture the developmental time line.

The phase of the campaign was from 1999 to 2000 and called 'Giving children back their future'. One image from the campaign showed a baby with a syringe ready to inject an illegal drug, with text that stated 'Battered as a child it was always possible John would turn to drugs. With Barnardo's help child abuse need not lead to an empty future.' The second part of the campaign was called 'Emotional death'. One of the adverts from this part portrayed a similarly hazardous situation; however, in this instance the person portrayed is an adult. You can see an adult depicted slumped in an armchair (presumably dead) with text stating 'Barry Stark. Died: Age 2 years'. The final part of the campaign was called 'Stolen childhood'. O'Dell (2008, p. 387) states of this phase: 'Here the child is again juxtaposed against a backdrop of an adult, hazardous context; however, each depiction is portraying a child in a situation designed to be read as a sexual situation.' For instance, one of the images in this series showed a young girl sitting on the side of a bed whilst a man was standing behind her; however the girl's face and hair had been digitally altered so she appeared aged. Whilst in the first and second campaigns, links were made showing how a child's start in life impacted on their future, the final campaign demonstrated the stark contrast between children and the adult situations they were being subjected to. The caption of the final image read 'Abuse through prostitution STEALS CHILDREN'S LIVES help end this obscenity.'

O'Dell (2008) argues that there are instances where pictures and text of the advertisements seek to elicit readers' concern for abused children by portraying them (a) as passive agents in their development and (b) as signifiers of the dangers of the world and the safeness of the home. She believes 'the portrayal of abused children in the advertisements serves to reinforce a perception of the vulnerability of all children and the need for adult supervision and "care"' (O'Dell, 2008, p. 383).

However, a later Barnardo's campaign, from 2003, generated more complaints than any other national press campaign (i.e. not on television, but in newspapers) in the ASA's history, and the ASA did decide that 'the charity had used unduly shocking images to attract attention and that the photographs used were likely to cause serious or widespread offence' in a campaign intended to draw attention to child poverty, with an image of cockroaches crawling out of a newborn baby's mouth. Barnardo's themselves say about their campaigns that:

> Unfortunately, the elements of our advertising that may seem disturbing to some people are everyday occurrences for many of the children and young people we work with. While we realise that this is hard to see, we feel it is important to reflect the true experiences of our service users, so that people understand that this is the sad reality for many children in the UK. We need to raise awareness of this, to prevent this happening to more children and young people. Although we do recognise our advertising can be hard-hitting, in no way is it intended to cause offence or distress. Instead, we want people to recognise that with intervention through organisations such as Barnardo's, things can change.
>
> (Barnardo's, 2016)

**TABLE 6.1** Jones' (2009) emerging and traditional attitudes to children

| Emerging view<br>The child as: | | Traditional approach<br>The child as: |
|---|---|---|
| capable | rather than | incapable |
| active | rather than | passive |
| visible | rather than | invisible |
| powerful | rather than | vulnerable and needy |
| valued and attended to in the present | rather than | seen and attended to as an investment for the future |
| an individual with their own capacities | rather than | a mini-adult lacking in full adult capacities |

Since the campaign of the early 2000s, Barnardo's have changed their approach to charity adverts and how children are portrayed in them. The latest campaign is called 'Believe In Me' and explores how children have been able to work through the difficulties they have faced, such as physical and sexual abuse, with the charity's support. Instead of showing children as vulnerable, powerless and incapable, children are instead portrayed as powerful, capable and strong. The advertising agency behind the campaign, FCB Inferno, states how they 'ripped up the rulebook of children's charity advertising, eschewing sad eyes and sorrow filled music for something far more powerful' (FCB Inferno, 2021).

This shift in how children are portrayed in Barnardo's charity adverts mirrors how the way that children are seen has shifted, which is something that we began to consider in Chapter 1 (*Children's media lives*) when we thought about the shift in seeing children's media usage as being comprised of **active**, rather than **passive**, activities. Jones (2009, p. 30) talks about how traditionally children have been seen as passive and incapable, whereas there is an emerging view of children as active and capable. Likewise, James and Prout (2003, p. 8) describe the emergent paradigm as viewing children as active agents in their own lives rather than the 'passive subjects of social structures and processes' that they may typically have been perceived as. Part of this shift has come about as a result of the United Nations Convention on the Rights of the Child (UNCRC), which has changed the way in which under 18s are seen worldwide, and their rights to protection, provision and participation. Jones (2009) presents a table (Table 6.1) that shows the differences in how children have been and are now viewed.

## Time to consider

Have a look at Table 6.1, which is Jones' description of the way children have been and are now seen. Take some time to watch some television adverts and note the ones that feature children. Which of these adjectives describes the way in which the children in the advertisements are portrayed?

## Final reflection

We come across advertisements every day, whether they are in print or on screen. What is significant about advertising is that it is typically not something that children choose to spend time engaging with, yet adverts permeate all kinds of their media usage. Advertising plays a role in the commercialisation and sexualisation of children. It also plays a role in the ways that children may be portrayed, and thus viewed and treated, by wider society. Children themselves acknowledge that there are adverts that make them feel uncomfortable, and Reg Bailey's review acknowledges that we need to think about how children are consumers and how advertising regulations reflects their views and wishes. As Bailey suggests, we cannot shield children indefinitely from the commercialisation of the twenty-first-century world, but we also cannot teach children to accept the status quo. Instead, what is needed is a fine balance of protection and information for children, with adults working together to ensure children aren't exposed to inappropriate advertising but also to support their ability to critique the marketing campaigns they may encounter.

## Key points

- We need to think carefully about the impact of advertising on children. Bailey (2013) suggests we need to 'let children be children' and be wary of the commercialisation and sexualisation of childhood.
- Both parents and children have a lot to say about advertising and how it may affect children. Some adverts that children are bothered by include violent adverts, those with sexual content, those that portray an idealised body image and charity adverts.
- It is important to think about how children are portrayed in adverts. In some adverts, for example charity adverts, children have traditionally been portrayed as vulnerable victims, although now some adverts are representing children as powerful.

## Further reading

1. O'Dell, L. (2008) 'Representations of the "Damaged" Child: "Child Saving" in a British Children's Charity Ad Campaign', *Children and Society*, 22(5), pp. 383–392.It is definitely worth having a read of O'Dell's piece of research that explores the portrayal of children in a series of Barnardo's advertisements. When reading it, think about how the way in which children are shown in the adverts could have an impact on how people view and treat them.

2. Bailey, R. (2011) *Letting Children Be Children: Report of an Independent Review of the Commercialisation and Sexualisation of Childhood*. Available at: www.gov.uk/government/uploads/system/uploads/attachment_data/file/175418/Bailey_Review.pdf (accessed 11 September 2021).Reg Bailey's report *Letting Children Be Children* is valuable to consider, despite the fact he made his recommendations over ten years ago now. His review gives critical insights into what a wide range of organisations and individuals believe about the commercialisation and sexualisation of childhood in the UK and what he believes should be done to counter this. When reading it, think about what, if anything, has changed in the time since he wrote this report.
3. Lupton D. (2014) 'Precious, Pure, Uncivilised, Vulnerable: Infant Embodiment in Australian Popular Media', *Children and Society*, 28(5), pp. 341–351. DOI: http://dx.doi.org/10.1111/chso.12004.This is a lovely study which examines how Australian television, newspaper and magazine advertisements and also newspaper and news magazine articles portray children aged under 2.

## References


Advertising Standards Authority (2012) *Public Perceptions of Harm and Offence in UK Advertising*. Available at: www.asa.org.uk/asset/DDB37644-FE4C-448E-9EC6F17E1DD1DF5D/ (accessed 11 March 2020).

Bailey, R. (2011) *Letting Children Be Children: Report of an Independent Review of the Commercialisation and Sexualisation of Childhood*. Available at: www.gov.uk/government/uploads/system/uploads/attachment_data/file/175418/Bailey_Review.pdf (accessed 11 March 2020).

Barnardo's (2016) *Advertising: Student FAQs*. www.barnardos.org.uk:80/advertising_students_faq (accessed 11 January 2016, webpage no longer available).

Blum-Ross, A. and Livingstone, S. (2016) *Families and Screen Time: Current Advice and Emerging Research*. Available at: http://eprints.lse.ac.uk/66927/1/Policy%20Brief%2017-%20Families%20%20Screen%20Time.pdf (accessed 11 March 2020).

Buckingham, D. (2005) 'Constructing the "Media Competent" Child: Media Literacy and Regulatory Policy in the UK', *MedienPädagogik: Zeitschrift für Theorie und Praxis der Medienbildung*, 11, pp. 1–14. https://doi.org/10.21240/mpaed/11/2005.09.27.X.

Campaign for a Commercial-Free Childhood (2020) *What Is a Commercial-Free Childhood*. Available at: https://commercialfreechildhood.org/commercialfree/ (accessed 11 March 2020).

Childnet International (2015) *Young people's experiences with in-app purchases*. Available at: www.childnet.com/ufiles/Young-people's-experiences-of-in-app-purchases.pdf (accessed 24 August 2021).

Committee of Advertising Practice (CAP) (2021) *Recognition of Advertising: Online Marketing to Children under 12 Advertising Guidance*. Available at: www.asa.org.uk/asset/27DBEBF0-6EEB-4E49-A44173CC8A9F5451.2F38244B-29EA-4830-85B5A5D65E4CA6C6/ (accessed 10 August 2021).

Department for Education (2013) *Letting Children Be Children: Progress Report*. Available at: www.gov.uk/government/uploads/system/uploads/attachment_data/file/203333/Bailey_Review_Progress_Report.pdf (accessed 14 December 2017).

FCB Inferno (2021) *Believe In Me*. Available at: www.fcbinferno.com/work/case-studies/believe-in-me/ (accessed 29 August 2021).

Fielder, A., Gardner, W., Nairn, A. and Pitt, J. (2007) *Fair Game? Assessing Commercial Activity on Children's Favourite Websites and Online Environments*. London: NCC.

Financial Conduct Authority (2021) *Financial Lives 2020 Survey: The Impact of Coronavirus*. Available at: www.fca.org.uk/publications/research/financial-lives-2020-survey-impact-coronavirus (accessed 24 August 2021).

Guldberg, H. (2009) *Reclaiming Childhood: Freedom and Play in an Age of Fear*. Abingdon: Routledge.

James, A. and Prout, A. (2003) *Constructing and Reconstructing Childhood*. London: FalmerPress.

Jones, P. (2009) *Rethinking Childhood: Attitudes in Contemporary Society*. London: Continuum.

Lupton D. (2014) 'Precious, Pure, Uncivilised, Vulnerable: Infant Embodiment in Australian Popular Media', *Children and Society*, 28(5), pp. 341–351. DOI: http://dx.doi.org/10.1111/chso.12004.

Millwood Hargrave, A. and Livingstone, S. (2009) *Harm and Offence in Media Content: A Review of the Evidence*, 2nd ed. Bristol: Intellect.

Nairn, A. and Dew, A. (2007) 'Pop-ups, Pop-unders, Banners and Buttons: The Ethics of Online Advertising to Primary School Children', *Journal of Direct, Data and Digital Marketing Practice*, 9, pp. 30–46.

Nunn, H. (2004) 'Emotional Death: The Charity Advert and Photographs of Childhood Trauma', *Journal for Cultural Research*, 8(3), pp. 271–292. DOI: 10.1080/1479758042000264948.

O'Dell, L. (2008) 'Representations of the "Damaged" Child: "Child Saving" in a British Children's Charity Ad Campaign', *Children and Society*, 22(5), pp. 383–392.

CHAPTER

7

# Innocent, invisible or feral

## Constructions of children in the media

## Introduction

Scan the newspaper stands and note how each newspaper screams 'Pick me! Pick me!' Carefully chosen photographs adorn the front pages vying for our attention; their accompanying headlines are guaranteed to evoke our empathy, our anger, or our curiosity. We are surrounded with images every moment of our lives and including images of children. We may use professional magazines or professional websites; perhaps we read the newspaper online or catch up with a lifestyle magazine. We might look for photos to illustrate a leaflet for parents or a resource we are making for children to use. All the while, we are surrounded by images, yet do we ever question how we interpret these images, the assumptions we make about children and the impact these images may have on us? Are we able to look at them critically? In addition to visual images, the media also uses the written word to illustrate childhood and tell us what we should think about children. Journalists carefully use language to invoke fear ('Camorra Child Gangsters Replace Omertà with Social Media Boasting', *The Guardian*, 2019), pity ('Betrayed: 1,800 Children Victims of Cruelty and Sex Assaults', *The Mirror*, 2021) or judgement ('"Addict" Three-Year-Old Boy Uses iPad Seven Hours a Day', *The Sun*, 2016).

In this chapter we are going to explore how children are constructed in the media through images and words; we will do this by considering how children are portrayed generally, but we also focus on several high-profile cases which are noteworthy in terms of how children are viewed. We will question why and how the media choose to depict certain children in certain ways and consider how this construction can impact on beliefs about children in wider society. The effect on children's socialisation will be discussed, for example, whether predominantly portraying them as victims leads to them becoming overprotected, or whether a thread of intolerance shown towards them throughout the media leads to them being misunderstood and unsupported. In addition, we will examine evidence that highlights how children feel about their portrayal. We will also

 DOI: 10.4324/9781003121206-9

reflect on the additional impact on the adults who care for children, work with children and have responsibility for them, people such as parents, social workers and teachers. We will consider whether portrayals of children then impact on their parents, being viewed as deficit and wanting, and certain professions, such as social work, being demonised. We will question the responsibility of journalism to examine how it contributes to harmful stereotypes.

## How are children portrayed in the media?

You flick through a magazine or scroll through an online newspaper; no doubt you will come across some photos of children that might make you think 'How sweet?', but are all children portrayed in the same way? The pages of my newspaper today have just one image, possibly demonstrating the low value of children to journalists who write for this particular paper. The photo shows three children in school uniform playing in a school playground. They are just being children, in the right place at the right time, doing what they should be doing. Yet the portrayal of children in media images is not always as straightforward as this. A quick glance at the home page of a different kind of newspaper shows several shots of babies on the hips of their celebrity mothers. If you were to analyse photographs and images of children presented in the media, you would realise that they are not presented in straightforward ways; rather their presentation 'reflects the complex and often contradictory ways in which adults can both portray and react to children' (Elsley, 2010, p. 10). This means that sometimes they may be portrayed as 'victims' yet conversely at other times as 'evil' (ibid.).

## The metaphorical child

The media has played a key role in the narratives and stories that surround children who have encountered tragic life events. For example, the tone of their reporting on the events that overtook Milly Dowling (murdered on her way home from school), Shannon Matthews (kidnapped in a plot that involved her own mother) and Peter Connelly (murdered by parents due to lack of failure to intervene by social workers), to name just three, impacted not only on the way that these children were viewed, but on how those who were involved in their lives were portrayed. These children became more than their name, they became what Warner (2014) terms 'the metaphorical child'. In the case of Baby P (as Peter Connelly was known in the press), this stands for all other children who have suffered or not been protected. The media, by their choice of headline and use of vocabulary, suggest how the public should feel (angry) and what steps should be taken ('Heads must roll') (Warner, 2014).

## The different ways that the media portrays children

All newspapers have political leanings, certain agendas they are trying to promote and certain audiences they are appealing to; however, the majority employ journalists who have a more privileged background than the average person. Jones (2020) notes how most journalists are from privileged backgrounds and therefore have little understanding of lives removed from their own. His book *Chavs: The Demonization of the Working Class* illustrates this point clearly by drawing on two cases of missing children which occurred within a year of each other. Both cases, Madeleine McCann in 2007 and then Shannon Matthews in 2008, became high-profile, although, Jones argues, for very different reasons. He suggests that Madeleine's disappearance struck a chord with middle-class journalists who identified with Madeleine's middle-class parents who lived a middle-class lifestyle, 'people just like us' (p. 14), as Jones quotes one journalist as saying. The result of this 'chord' was extended media involvement and generous financial donations. This reaction contrasted greatly with the disappearance of Shannon Matthews, who provoked little interest in the media until her mother was implicated in her disappearance. Suddenly, there was an overwhelmingly negative and sustained focus on their northern working-class community, described offensively by one journalist as 'an underclass which is a world apart from the lives that most of us lead and the attitudes and social conventions that most of us take for granted' (p. 18).

These contrasting portrayals of two children and their families illustrate how children are rarely depicted in a neutral manner in the press; it seems there must always be an agenda. They are positioned in a way to emphasise their place in society, they are used for political gain and they are exploited to line the pockets of others.

## Time to consider

Think about Warner's concept of the metaphorical child and reflect on how the image of one child could be used to 'touch on profound social, cultural and political anxieties' (2014, p. 1638). Now gather some images of children; you may find it easier to do this electronically. You can focus on one publication, such as a professional publication like *Nursery World*, or you could look at a group of reports such as those published by Ofsted or a charity. After selecting several images, consider who is the metaphorical child that they are trying to depict? To help your thinking process you could annotate the images with some descriptive words, both to describe the child/children and to document how they make you feel. Now compare your thoughts with others who have carried out the same process; are there common themes or disagreements? Are we all being told similar stories about children or are we using the filter of our experiences to arrive at a narrative?

## What is the impact on children, parents, and professionals?

It is not surprising that, when consulted, children are clear that they are not happy about the way they are portrayed in the media. For example, the 'See it, Say it, Change it' project worked with children 7 to 18 years old to find out their views on their rights and, in particular, their perspectives on the way that the media promotes stereotypes about them (CRAE, 2015, p. 4). Children were very clear that they were not happy with how they were represented in the media, saying, 'Media stereotypes teenagers especially as badly behaving troublemakers which makes a lot of people look at us like we are dirt' (Female, 16, p. 11). Another boy of 10 observed, 'sometimes they can be disrespectful about age and sometimes they don't listen to children as well as they do to adults' (p. 11), and yet another girl of 12, 'they say that children are horrid vicious things when we are not' (p. 11).

The vocabulary used by these children may appear emotive and somewhat extreme, yet these children are supported in their viewpoints by evidence from the United Nations who agree with the children's objections. In their 2016 report on the rights of children in the UK, they reiterated a 'previous recommendation that the State party take urgent measures to address the "intolerance of childhood" and general negative public attitude towards children, especially adolescents, within society, including in the media' (Committee for the Rights of the Child, 2016).

The evidence suggests that not only are children aware of how they are portrayed in the media, but that they also are not happy with this portrayal. They have absorbed the prevailing 'intolerance of childhood' which surrounds them through images and the printed word. Furthermore, their voice is often missing, and surprisingly so when children's rights are being discussed.

## The portrayal of parents

Parents are also portrayed in the same contradictory manner as their children by the media. On the one hand, they are victims of the tyrannical rule of their children who drive them to drink through their difficult behaviour (Mesure, 2016). They are unsupported by inflexible schools with inflexible rules which mean their children are sent home if they have the wrong haircut or the wrong shoes (Flaherty, 2020). Their children hit them (Phillips and Bell, 2015), use their credit cards (Kleinman, 2019), require a personalised menu (Rumack and Tansey, 2015) and are uncontrollable (Carr, 2021). At the same time, some more famous parents are held up to the spotlight, not only to show what wonderful, caring, nurturing parents they are, think of the Duchess of Cambridge, but also how supportive they are of other struggling parents, who need help and encouragement to be as magnificent at the job as they are. Celebrities provide parenting blogs, books and podcasts to share their wisdom and parenting skills (Giovanna Fletcher, *Happy*

*Mum, Happy Baby* (2017); Sam Faiers *My Baby and Me*, (2016); Holly Willoughby, *Truly Happy Baby: It Worked for Me*, (2016). Yet elsewhere parents are criticised for overparenting (Lascala, 2019) and thus engendering a generation of children with little resilience who cannot fend for themselves; really, if we focus on their portrayal within the media, parents just can't win.

## The 'blame the parent' thread

The overwhelming message is that the ills of society are the fault of parents and particularly those parents described by David Cameron as 'fighting a losing battle against degradation' and living in 'drug and crime-ridden communit[ies]' (Thornton, 2009), as he referenced the Shannon Matthews case. The message implies that if these parents are not taken to task by being controlled, and then in return learning to control their children, then society will continue down a broken path to terrible outcomes. To address fear, Cameron's government announced a voucher scheme (Boffey, 2016) for parenting lessons. Controversially, Cameron also included single parent families in his list of problematic family issues and their impact on wider society: 'Irresponsibility. Selfishness. Behaving as if your choices have no consequences. Children without fathers. Schools without discipline. Reward without effort' (Stratton, 2011). This additional demonisation of single mothers, which positioned them as incapable of being effective parents, did not align with findings of research studies (see for example Golombok et al. 2016). Nevertheless, perceived gaps in parents' understanding, skills and effectiveness have led to a whole 'parenting industry' springing up (Gopnik, 2016).

## The parenting industry

Parenting has certainly become big business, rather than an activity which traditionally involved not just the immediate parent(s) but also the extended family, who were on hand to provide childcare, support and advice. Instead, parents in the twenty-first century are required to turn to books by celebrity parents, podcasts, websites, and TV programmes. There is a suggestion that 'this media hype regarding aspects of parenting' (Simmons, 2020, p. 93) has led to mothers in particular feeling 'judged in their mother role' (ibid.).

Parents, as well as their offspring, are subject to the whims of the press in terms of whether society sees them as strong competent leaders of future generations, or weak role models with no clear moral code to adhere to. Parents, in addition to their children, are not allowed just to 'be'; instead, they have to be portrayed, positioned, caricatured and demonised. The media delights in presenting parents in the same binary way that they present children: parents are either 'feckless, welfare-scrounging begetters of feral yobs, teenage mums and vandals' or 'hard-working, middle Englanders ... whose lives are presumed to be ruined by their less responsible peers' (Millar, 2007, p. 47). Regardless, there is a strong 'blame the parent' thread that runs through their portrayal, a thread which lets others off the hook in terms of their responsibilities towards young children. Parents feel the weight of this blame on their shoulders and are eager consumers of the resources provided by the ever developing parenting industry.

## The portrayal of professionals

### Social workers

Social workers are seldom portrayed in the media in a complimentary way; usually it is a perceived incompetence and unprofessional behaviour that are highlighted. The media, by their choice of headline and use of vocabulary, often suggest how the public should feel towards them (angry) and how they should be treated ('Heads must roll') (Warner, 2014). The social workers involved in the case of Baby P were stereotyped as 'inept or politically correct busy bodies' (Fraser, 2004, cited in Jones, 2012, p. 84).

### Teachers

Teachers too have grown to be wary of their treatment by, and depiction in, the media. We could suggest that there are not so many extremes in their depiction compared to social workers, although there have been periods when it was wise not to admit you were a teacher, for instance as the media reported on teacher strikes or teacher pensions; as a profession, teachers are hardly viewed in a neutral way. Then there are those who work with the youngest children in an early years setting ....

### Early years practitioners

The way that early years practitioners are depicted speaks volumes about how they are considered as unimportant, doing an unimportant job with very young children who are not worthy of consideration. For example, they were repeatedly omitted from media discussions throughout the pandemic and little consideration was given to their fears as they continued as key workers, whilst health professionals were clapped weekly from people's doorsteps and hailed, quite rightly, as heroes.

The demonisation and deficit view of those who work with young children reflects the media's contradictory positioning of childhood. On the one hand, these vulnerable tiny creatures need adults who can protect them, yet on the other hand those perceived to be in this role can be depicted, at best, as low skilled and at worst as incompetent or lazy.

## Time to consider

Think about the responsibility of journalists toward children, and their important adults, and the ways they are portrayed in the media. The International Federation of Journalists (IFJ) (2003, p. 3) sets out the positive impact that journalists can have if they adopt a more ethical, less binary or sensationalist portrayal of children in their work. The Accountable Journalism project draws on the IFJ's work to set out some of the issues which surround children's portrayal in the media, issues such as:

- children living in poverty ... lose their individuality and humanity. They are often portrayed as helpless sufferers, unable to act, think or speak for themselves.
- Coverage of children's issues tends to focus on the sensational while ignoring the broad array of issues confronting children, as outlined in the Convention on the Rights of the Child.
- Media reports about children are often one-off stories, with little or no analysis or follow-up.
- Children's confidentiality is not always respected.
- When children do feature in the news, they are often portrayed as stereotypes such as 'starving children in Africa' and 'irresponsible teenagers'.

(Accountable Journalism, n.d.)

Consider these issues in the light of media reporting on the cases of Madeleine McCann or Shannon Matthews. If journalists had considered these, what might the impact have been and how might the reporting have differed?

# What is the impact on children's socialisation?

## A culture of fear

In 1997, Frank Furedi wrote a book entitled *Culture of Fear*; when he returned to this discussion of fear in 2018, he recognised how this little discussed concept had become a prominent part of our daily life in the twenty-first century. He also recognised the differences between how we fear in the present day and what fear would look like in the past. If you were to ask someone several generations older than yourself, you would see immediately that he has a point; whatever my own parents' generation worried about, they certainly did not fear allowing their children to roam freely. My friends and I recall in the 1960s and 1970s packing up sandwiches and then disappearing for a summer's day, with no parental concern at all as long as we were back for tea time. This was when we hadn't even reached double digits. It was interesting to revisit our old haunts recently, all of us using our twenty-first-century perspective to carry out a mental risk assessment of the activities we had engaged in, building fires, climbing down steep waterfalls and paddling in rivers. We concluded that we wondered how we had managed to survive.

## The bubble-wrap generation

Compare this picture with Malone's description of children in 2007, children she called 'the bubble-wrap generation' (Malone, 2007) whose 'parents are restricting children's movements to such an extent that these children do not have the social, psychological, or environmental knowledge and skills to be able to negotiate freely in the environment' (p. 513). Malone was writing in the context of Australia and she draws on both her own research with 50 children, aged 4 to 8 years, and that of others to make her claims. Her own study invited these 50 children to capture through photographs 'the places they went and activities they engaged' in (p. 516) over the course of a week. She was astounded to see that 'at least half included a picture of driving in the back seat of the car' (p. 517). Malone was writing over a decade ago, however if we skip forward to 2019, we find that Love et al. (2020) note, 'Research has documented the decline in children's independent mobility (CIM) globally.' Their finding is echoed elsewhere such as in an international comparison of CIM across 16 countries including 18,303 children aged between 7 and 15 years old (Shaw et al., 2015).

We asked if children were too safe for their own good at the beginning of this section; this is a highly complex question to answer and must be considered within the context of Furedi's culture of fear. Such fear leads adults, whether they be parents, carers or professionals, to be perhaps more vigilant than necessary in a desire to keep children in their care safe. This concern is clearly illustrated in the freedom, or lack of, for children to roam and explore independently.

We can clearly see a link between the notion of a culture of fear and the concept of bubble-wrapped children. We are extra careful with things we fear may break easily and it seems that now this extra care extends to even our children. Yet parents are not only fearful, they may also be confused; the media offers confusing messages about how protective we should be of young children. On the one hand, the media suggests that it has never been a more dangerous time to be a child because of 'stranger danger', a danger that has intensified because of the opportunities offered by technology to those who would wish children harm. On the other hand, we are warned of the dangers of overprotecting them. Lindon, in her book *Too Safe for Their Own Good?* (2011), describes how the media 'swings between two extremes' of 'lurid headlines that frighten many families into being highly protective' and blaming parents for 'creating a generation of couch potatoes' (p. 2).

## Children and the concept of risk

We can link the idea of risk-taking behaviour to the idea of children as vulnerable. If adults are fearful about what will happen to the children in their care then they will not only limit how far they can wander away from it, but they will also restrict what they can do even when they are near them, so this could include how they police children's engagement with media. Hypervigilant adults have 'a substantial impact on child well-being, [and their] mental health … [including] low self-esteem and early onset obesity' (Pizzo et al., 2021). Pizzo et al. describe overprotective parenting as being 'a parenting style characterized by removing children from potentially risky or threatening situations and providing a degree of help during challenging tasks, which is excessive'. Parental anxiety is also 'associated with increased cortisol levels in children' (Fields et al., 2021, p. 15). So anxious parents will not only discourage children from adopting healthy and appropriate risk-taking behaviours, they will also encourage children to independently choose to shy away from them. And this is not only limited to early childhood – an important point if we consider assertions around the period of childhood and how it appears to be continually lengthening.

Lindon (2011) ruminates on how the period of childhood appears to be lasting even longer than it ever did. Scientists echo this in findings that the period of adolescence, which Sawyer et al. (2018) define as 'biological growth and major social role transitions', is different from that of 100 years ago as:

> delayed timing of role transitions, including completion of education, marriage, and parenthood, continue to shift popular perceptions of when adulthood begins. Arguably, the transition period from childhood to adulthood now occupies a greater portion of the life course than ever before at a time when unprecedented social forces, including marketing and digital media, are affecting health and wellbeing across these years.

They continue by advising that 'a definition of 10–24 years corresponds more closely to adolescent growth and popular understandings of this life phase'.

Lindon is concerned that, in parallel to this extension of the journey into becoming an adult, 'the world of children has become more separate from that of adults' and that this gap between the two worlds has led to children being protected from risk-taking behaviours which would support their growth into skilled adults. She goes on to describe the limitations that are placed on children in terms of them developing practical life skills. This is an opposing argument to that of Postman, that we will look at in Chapter 8 (*Helpful theoretical lenses: how theory can help us understand children's engagement with the media*), who talks about how our access to information is leading towards the disappearance of childhood.

## Time to consider

There are many tensions both for parents and for all those who work with children in how they should treat them and what they should take into consideration in their interactions with them. On the one hand, the media continually reminds us what a dangerous place the world is for children to live in, and on the other, we are reminded that children need to learn about risk and that overprotecting them prevents them from developing into skilled and independent adults. To what extent do you think viewing children as vulnerable in twenty-first-century Britain impacts on how we treat them?

## Final reflection

In this chapter we have explored the power that the media has in influencing the way that children are perceived in society; there is a power imbalance in that children do not have agency in the way that they are portrayed. These portrayals are social constructions rather than absolute truths; the specific constructions of particular types of children are influenced by a variety of factors including class, socioeconomic status, geographical context and particular media outlets' affiliations. It is important to consider how children perceive the way they are constructed in the press and the negative impact on their lives because of issues of socialisation. It would be good to reflect at this point on what might be done to change the way that children are presented in the media, including prevalent perspectives of children that are found there. We need to question our role as advocates in doing this, but also consider how we might support children both to understand and to challenge the stereotypes about them that are shared in the popular press.

## Key points

- Children are presented in contradictory ways in the international media; for example, they can be seen as innocent and vulnerable, yet on the other hand they can be portrayed as having little value, delinquent and to be feared. This depiction of their lives may lead children to feel confused, powerless and misunderstood.
- The negative impact of this portrayal impacts not only on the individual child but also on their parents, carers, and professionals who work with them.
- Children's socialisation is affected by very many different factors, yet the powerful influence of the media cannot be denied; children see themselves reflected in advertisements, news headlines and films.

## Further reading

1. Warner, J. (2014) '"Heads Must Roll"? Emotional Politics, the Press and the Death of Baby P.', *British Journal of Social Work*, 44, pp. 1637–1653.This article examines newspapers' role in demonising social workers following the tragic case of Baby P.
2. Jones, O. (2020) *Chavs: The Demonization of the Working Class*. London: Verso. Read in particular chapter 1, 'The Strange Case of Shannon Matthews', to understand further the media's response to the disappearance of both Shannon Matthews and Madeleine McCann.
3. Children's Rights Alliance for England (CRAE) (2015) *See it, Say it, Change it*. Available at: www.crae.org.uk/media/78664/crae_seeit-sayit-changeit_web.pdf (accessed 4 September 2019). This project worked with children aged 7 to 18 years to find out their views on their rights. Chapter 1, 'Respect', looks in particular at how the media exacerbates intolerant attitudes towards children.

## References


Accountable Journalism (n.d.) *Child Rights International Network: Discrimination and the Media*. Available at: https://accountablejournalism.org/ethics-codes/child-rights-international-network-discrimination (accessed 2 August 2021).

Boffey, D. (2016) 'David Cameron: Parents Should Be Taught How to Control Children'. Available at: www.theguardian.com/politics/2016/jan/10/david-cameron-parents-children-lessons (accessed 1 August 2021).

Carr, J. (2021) Generation of home-schooled children lacked 'discipline and order' during lockdown says Gavin Williamson as he backs mobile phone ban in schools and says 'out of control' pupils will wreck lessons. Available at: www.dailymail.co.uk/news/article-9443355/Home-schooled-children-lacked-discipline-order-lockdown-says-Gavin-Williamson.html (accessed 1 August 2021).

Children's Rights Alliance for England (CRAE) (2015) *See it, Say it, Change it*. Available at: www.crae.org.uk/media/78664/crae_seeit-sayit-changeit_web.pdf (accessed 15 August 2021).

Committee for the Rights of the Child (CRC) (2016) *Concluding Observations on the Fifth Periodic Report of the United Kingdom of Great Britain and Northern Ireland*. Available at: www.crae.org.uk/media/93148/UK-concluding-observations-2016.pdf (accessed 28 July 2021).

Elsley, S. (2010) *Media Coverage of Child Deaths in the UK: The Impact of Baby P: A Case for Influence?* Available at: www.research.ed.ac.uk/portal/files/13105529/K201009.pdf (accessed 15 August 2021).

Faiers, S. (2016) *My Baby and Me*. London: Bonnier Publishing Ltd.

Fields, A., Harman, C., Lee, Z., Louie, J. and Tottenham, N. (2021) 'Parent's Anxiety Links Household Stress and Young Children's Behavioral Dysregulation', *Developmental Psychobiology*, 63, pp. 16–30.

Flaherty, J. (2020) 'Kids Sent Home from School over Fake Tan, Haircuts and Shoes'. Available at: www.liverpoolecho.co.uk/news/liverpool-news/kids-sent-home-school-over-18914498 (accessed 1 August 2021).

Fletcher, G. (2017) *Happy Mum, Happy Baby*. London: Hachette UK.

Furedi, F. (1997) *Culture of fear*. London: Continuum.

Furedi, F. (2018) *How Fear Works*. London: Bloomsbury.

Golombok, S., Zadeh, S., Imrie, S., Smith, V. and Freeman, T. (2016) 'Single Mothers by Choice: Mother–Child Relationships and Children's Psychological Adjustment', *Journal of Family Psychology*, 30(4), pp. 409–418.

Gopnik, A. (2016) *The Gardener and the Carpenter*. New York: Random House.

The Guardian (2019) 'Camorra Child Gangsters Replace Omertà with Social Media Boasting'. Available at: www.theguardian.com/world/2019/feb/25/camorra-child-gangsters-replace-omerta-with-social-media-boasting (accessed 28 July 2021).

International Federation of Journalists (IFJ) (2003) *Telling Their Stories: Child Rights, Exploitation and the Media*.

Jones, O. (2020) *Chavs: The Demonization of the Working Class*. London: Verso.

Jones, R. (2012) 'Child Protection, Social Work and the Media: Doing as Well as Being Done to', *Research, Policy and Planning*, 29(2), pp. 83–94.

Jones, R. (2014) *The Story of Baby P: Setting the Record Straight*. Bristol: Polity Press.

Kleinman, Z. (2019) 'My Son Spent £3,160 in One Game'. Available at: www.bbc.co.uk/news/technology-48925623 (accessed 1 August 2021).

Lascala, M. (2019) *What Is Helicopter Parenting? Experts Say It's Too Much for Kids*. Available at: www.goodhousekeeping.com/life/parenting/a27044118/what-is-helicopter-parenting/ (accessed 1 August 2021).

Lindon, J. (2011) *Too Safe for Their Own Good?* London: NCB.

Love, P., Villanueva, K. and Whitzman, C. (2020) 'Children's Independent Mobility: The Role of School-Based Social Capital', *Children's Geographies*, 18(3), pp. 253–268.

Malone, K. (2007) 'The Bubble-Wrap Generation: Children Growing up in Walled Gardens', *Environmental Education Research*, 13(4), pp. 513–527.

Mesure, S. (2016) 'From Smug to Slummy: The Myths of Modern Parenthood'. Available at: www.theguardian.com/lifeandstyle/2016/sep/26/from-smug-to-slummy-the-myths-of-modern-parenthood (accessed 1 August 2021).

Millar, F. (2007) 'For the Sake of the Children', *British Journalism Review*, 18(1), pp. 45–49.

Mirror (2021) 'Betrayed: 1,800 Children Victims of Cruelty and Sex Assaults'. Available at: https://news.sky.com/story/wednesdays-national-newspaper-front-pages-12365823 (accessed 28 July 2021).

Phillips, N. and Bell, S. (2015) 'The Children Who Hit Their Parents'. Available at: https://www.bbc.co.uk/news/uk-34879818 (accessed 1 August 2021).

Pizzo, A., Sandstrom, A., Drobinin, V., Propper, L., Uher, R. and Pavlova, B. (2021) 'Parental Overprotection and Sleep Problems in Young Children', *Child Psychiatry & Human Development*. doi.org/10.1007/s10578-021-01199-2.

Rumack, L. and Tansey, C. (2015) *The debate: Do you make separate meals for your kids and for yourself?* Available at: www.todaysparent.com/family/parenting/do-you-make-separate-meals-for-your-kids-and-for-yourself/ (accessed 1 August 2021).

Sawyer, S., Azzopardi, P., Wickremarathne, D. and Patton, G. (2018) 'The Age of Adolescence', *The Lancet*, 3(3), pp. 223–228.

Shaw, B., Bicket, M., Elliott, B., Fagan-Watson, B., Mocca, E. and Hillman, M. (2015) *Children's Independent Mobility: An International Comparison and Recommendations for Action.* Available at: www.nuffieldfoundation.org/sites/default/files/files/7350_PSI_Report_CIM_final.pdf (accessed 15 August 2021).

Simmons, H. (2020) *Surveillance of Modern Motherhood: Experiences of Universal Parenting Courses.* London: Palgrave Macmillan.

Stratton, A. (2011) 'David Cameron on Riots: Broken Society Is Top of My Political Agenda'. Available at: www.theguardian.com/uk/2011/aug/15/david-cameron-riots-broken-society (accessed 1 August 2021).

The Sun (2016) '"Addict" Three-Year-Old Boy Uses iPad Seven Hours a Day'. Available at: www.thesun.co.uk/living/2244540/addict-three-year-old-boy-uses-gadget-seven-hours-a-dayand-his-mum-insists-its-good-for-him/ (accessed 28 July 2021).

Thornton, L. (2009) 'David Cameron Apologises to Shannon Matthews' Neighbours'. Available at: www.mirror.co.uk/news/uk-news/david-cameron-apologises-to-shannon-matthews-413674 (accessed 1 August 2021).

UNICEF (1989) *The United Nations Convention on the Rights of the Child.* Available at: unicef.org.uk. (accessed 15 August 2021).

United Nations Committee on the Rights of the Child (2016) *Concluding Observations on the Fifth Periodic Report of the United Kingdom of Great Britain and Northern Ireland.* Available at: www.crae.org.uk/media/93148/UK-concluding-observations-2016.pdf (accessed 15 August 2021).

Warner, J. (2014) '"Heads Must Roll"? Emotional Politics, the Press and the Death of Baby P.', *British Journal of Social Work*, 44, pp. 1637–1653.

Willoughby, H. (2016) *Truly Happy Baby: It Worked for Me.* London: HarperCollins.

CHAPTER

8

# Helpful theoretical lenses

## How theory can help us understand children's engagement with the media

## Introduction

Do you like to go to the theatre? Perhaps you love to go to musicals in London or you are lucky enough to have a theatre not too far from your home. Why are we talking about theatre here? You may remember in Chapter 1 (*Introduction*) we explained that our students often share anecdotal examples about children and their engagement with media. We also agreed that these examples were useful starting points but that our aim was to support you to think more critically about them. One of the ways we can do this is by looking at some useful theoretical lenses which may help us understand what is going on when children engage with media. That's where the word 'theatre' comes in. Both 'theory' and 'theatre' derive from the same Greek word which means to observe or contemplate (The Vocabularist, 2016). If you visit the theatre, you may pick your seat carefully because you know that your view of the stage is determined by your position in the auditorium. It is helpful to think of theorists in the same way; on the stage is a child playing with their first mobile but what the theorists actually see depends on where they are seated, i.e. where they are coming from.

## How can Bronfenbrenner help us understand children's media engagement?

Bronfenbrenner is a key thinker for those interested in early childhood. His ecological system theory has impacted greatly on the way that research into children and families is conducted, and how the findings of this research are translated into practice (Lang, 2005). Lang (2005) notes how Melvin L. Kohn, a professor of sociology and one of Bronfenbrenner's former students, describes

DOI: 10.4324/9781003121206-10

how he made psychologists 'realize that interpersonal relationships, even the smallest level of the child and the parent-child relationship, did not exist in a social vacuum but were embedded in the larger social structures of community, society, economics, and politics'. As Lang sets out Bronfenbrenner's extraordinary contribution, she explains that 'before [him], child psychologists studied the child, sociologists examined the family, anthropologists the society, economists the economic framework of the times and political scientists the structure'. Bronfenbrenner understood that child development was complex and nuanced; psychologists also failed to explore the interactions between the different contexts of the child. We have argued elsewhere about the limitations of Early Childhood research carried out in 'artificial laboratory environments' (Bolshaw and Josephidou, 2018, p. 57), which does not take children's own experiences into account and is 'unidirectional' (Rosa and Tudge, 2013, p. 249), i.e. it considers the impact of the variable on the child but not the child on the variable.

## The ecological systems theory

Bronfenbrenner described the contexts of the child as four different systems; he gave each system a name depending on its proximity to the child. Table 8.1 sets out the systems along with their definitions.

Although Bronfenbrenner was known for this seminal theory, he was also very concerned with its practical application (Tudge et al., 2021). This was demonstrated by his contribution to the Head Start initiative. It is important to note that Bronfenbrenner (1994) continued to develop his theory and instead named it the 'Bioecological model'. He set out his development of the ecological model into the bioecological model in a paper written with Ceci (1994) to emphasise the role of the interaction between the individual's genes and their environment, an interaction that had not been foregrounded in his original ecological model.

**TABLE 8.1** Ecological systems theory (adapted from Jordan, 2005, p. 526)

| Context | Definition | Examples |
|---|---|---|
| Microsystem | Child's day-to-day setting | Family; peers; teachers |
| Mesosystem | Relationships or intersections between microsystems | How the early childhood setting reflects the values of the home environment |
| Exosystem | Social settings in which the child does not have a direct role | Parents' occupation; **the media** |
| Macrosystem | Broader cultural context | Ethnicity; historical setting |

## Using Bronfenbrenner's lens to understand children and the media

Jordan (2005) uses Bronfenbrenner's ideas to understand young children's interactions with the media. She states:

> we can trace children's experiences with books and television from the home to the center (the microsystem), parental stresses that might encourage or discourage the use of media in particular ways (the exosystem), the convergence (or divergence) of messages children receive about media from these contexts (the mesosystem), and the cultural patterns that shape expectations about uses for media (the macrosystem).
>
> (Jordan, 2005, p. 525)

Her work examined the reading and television habits of young children and suggests, from her data, the importance of 'books, television, and videotapes' in their lives. Although she concluded that these media sources were used very differently by practitioners; for example, television took up more time in the setting, it was 'driven by children's interests' and it was used as a transition device. Let us now look at further research which has focused on the specific systems within Bronfenbrenner's theory.

## The microsystem

Jago et al. (2012) looked at the amount of time children spent engaging with screens, because of concerns raised about the impact of screen time on health outcomes. They wanted to find out how both parents' screen time and children's access to media impacted on children's screen time. They were researching in the context of Portugal and their participants were 2,965 Portuguese families with children aged 3–10 years. They found a strong association between the amount of time parents spent watching television and children's amount of screen time, in particular if this was the mother.

## The mesosytem

Selwyn et al. (2011) investigated how schools support parents to in turn support their child's learning through virtual learning platforms. Their work was in the context of England and they carried out case studies in 12 schools, half of which were primary and half secondary. As well as considering this practice from the schools' perspective they wanted to find out what the parents' views and understanding were. The findings reveal that using technology in this way to engage with parents is not without its problems and tensions. Although some parents did appreciate the opportunities this offered, very many were either unaware or uninterested. The authors suggest that this type of technological interaction is 'part of the "mutual surveillance" that characterizes the contemporary parent/school relationship' (p. 322). They argue that this kind of technology did not bring anything new to the parent/school relationship, rather it reinforced that already in place.

## The exosystem

You probably recall how in Chapter 7 (*Innocent, invisible or feral: Constructions of children in the media*) we discussed the portrayal of social workers in the media. In Davies' work (2014) she explores the different ways social workers look to work with the media to best protect children. Speaking from her own professional experience as a social worker, she argues that this is an important relationship as 'Without investigative journalism and persistent media coverage, the perpetrators would not … [be] exposed or reported to police' (p. 47). She goes on to praise the dedication of certain journalists, and states that this relationship with the media provides 'a strong and influential voice in seeking justice for abused children', at the same time as providing a different perspective from the one we depicted in Chapter 7 that set out the deficit presentation of social workers in the media.

## The macrosystem

Finally, let us look at some research that considers the context of the macrosystem in young children's lives. Pires et al. (2015) considered the macro context of Brazilian society and what children within it think about smoking, because of concerns that those children who are introduced to cigarettes at 7 plus have an increased probability of becoming regular smokers as adults. They worked with 5–6-year-old children (n = 398) in Brazil and used photos of smokers and non-smokers as a prompt for interviews, logos of cigarette brands to check for children's knowledge of these, and pictures of popular media characters to check children's exposure to the media. Based on their findings, they suggest that 'Shaped by social and environmental influences, very young children have opinions about smokers. In turn, these attitudes significantly predict children's smoking intentions' (p. 1124).

## Time to consider

Jordan (2004, p. 197) discusses why an ecological approach may be 'a useful paradigm for thinking about and studying how media shape children's development'. Why is this? Why do you think this might be the case? She refers to the policy and public concerns that exist about children's media use. However, this study is dated and from a US perspective. What evidence from other sources can you find to inform us about this from a UK perspective? Jordan (2004) finds evidence to support the role of media on children's (a) physical development, (b) social development and (c) school performance. Choose one area – what UK statistics or evidence can you find? Finally, Jordan (2004, p. 204) presents her recommendations for parents and caregivers, such as to make sure they know:

- what their children are watching (not just the title but the content)
- how much screen time they spend
- educational content they can direct their children to

Write your own list of 5–10 recommendations, using evidence to back them up.

## How can Bourdieu help us understand children's media engagement?

We are going to turn our attention now to another seminal thinker, Pierre Bourdieu, who was born in France in the 1930s. His work has been important in the discipline of sociology and, particularly, in educational research. Bourdieu gave us three key concepts to support our understanding of the impact of the media on young children's lives, although he was not writing specifically about the area of early childhood; these are the concepts of:

- habitus
- field
- forms of capital

Let's examine each of these ideas in turn.

### Habitus

In their book *Childhood with Bourdieu*, Alanen, Brooker and Mayall (2015) note how useful the lens of Bourdieu is. It is a helpful text to examine these key concepts in the context of early childhood. To define habitus, they draw on Bourdieu's own definition:

> Habitus is a set of dispositions, reflexes and forms of behaviour that people acquire through acting in society. It reflects the differing positions people have in society, for example, whether they are brought up in a middle class environment or in a working class suburb. It is part of how society reproduces itself.
>
> (Bourdieu, 2000, p. 19)

They conclude that 'Habitus is produced when people "internalise" the material, cultural and intellectual structures that constitute a particular type of environment' (Alanen, Brooker and Mayall, 2015, p. 6).

### Field

The term 'field' is the second key concept of Bourdieu's that is useful in supporting our understanding of young children's engagement with the media. Let us turn once again to Alanen, Brooker and Mayall (2015); they describe it, in the context specifically of childhood, as 'an arena, an environment, or a space in which childhood is under question' (p. 4). They give the example of 'the family' or the early childhood setting. So, a field can be a physical space, or it can be a social space, or it can be both of these at the same time. They further cite Bourdieu to explain that 'each field has its own rules, or logic, so the game and the rules of one field are different from the games and the rules in another field' (Bourdieu and Wacquant, 1992, pp. 94–115). They go on to suggest that 'all fields are structured by relations of dominance' (Alanen, Brooker and Mayall, 2015, p. 6).

In their chapter of this same book, 'Early Childhood Education as a Social Field', Vuorisalo and Alanen (2015) state the importance of observing interactions in the ECEC setting to gain an understanding of 'what is going on here' (p. 79). They depict a scene where a practitioner is interacting with young children, to illustrate the power relationships within this field; the practitioner is inconsistent in applying the rules of the setting, depending upon which children she is engaging with. Why do you think this might be?

## Capital

One reason for the practitioner's inconsistency could be the different forms of capital that the children possess (or not) as they navigate these fields, learning the rules of each and adopting the appropriate behaviours and dispositions in order to fit in. In particular, Bourdieu focuses on economic capital, cultural capital and social capital within his theoretical thinking. Let's look at each one of these in turn in Table 8.2: what exactly do these terms mean?

Bourdieu's ideas around the various forms of capital (economic, cultural and social) can lend us a helpful lens in understanding children's engagement with, and representation in, the media. Economic capital allows children to access the various forms of media in the first place. (Although there is a common criticism

**TABLE 8.2** Different forms of capital according to Bourdieu

| Form of capital | Meaning | Example in ECEC |
|---|---|---|
| Economic | The material and financial resources you have at your disposal | **A** doesn't like to play outside when she attends the setting; her hand-me-down shoes don't fit properly and the thin, worn soles make her slip if she tries to run. |
| Cultural | The way we signify our social class through mannerisms, the things we like, the things we are good at | **B** just has something about him the teacher finds it hard to like, whether it's the way he wipes his nose on his sleeve, constantly talks about wrestling he's watched on TV or his complete inability to contribute anything meaningful to group discussions. |
| Social | Opportunities to engage with others which support our own development | **C** was very worried about her child **D** starting school. She was particularly shy and quite young for her age. The other children had known **D** for all of their young lives so they took care of her and made sure she was okay. |

of families living in poverty accessing enormous television sets or having the latest mobile phones – is this actually the reality?) Cultural capital is seen in children engaging with the 'right kind' of media output – perhaps the newspapers their parents read (or not), the media output they are allowed to access and whether they see themselves represented there; whereas social capital can be seen in opportunities to engage with others through media channels. Although Bourdieu was writing many years ago, his ideas are still useful in the present-day context of early childhood. There has been renewed interest in his work, and its relevance to Early Childhood, in recent years as Ofsted has picked up on his concept of cultural capital with regard to how they evaluate the impact that ECEC settings should have. However, this is a contested phraseology in terms of how various stakeholders and interested parties interpret its meaning. For example, Ofsted define cultural capital as 'the essential knowledge that children need to be educated citizens' (Ofsted, 2019), but Palmer (2019) argues that interpretations of this definition can lead to practice which views the unique child in a deficit way, by looking to impose a type of culture rather than valuing the unique experiences and culture they bring to the setting.

### Time to consider

#### The case of *Frozen*

When the Disney film *Frozen* was released, it caused a storm in terms of young children's reaction (Lynskey, 2014). Children watched the DVD over and over, persuaded parents to buy the associated merchandise, learnt the songs off by heart and, in the words of one practitioner, 'all they want to do is play Frozen'. A group of practitioners from a variety of settings were discussing this phenomenon as part of their higher studies. Some felt it was important to let the children continue to play this way and to meet their requests for appropriate resources to enhance their play. Others felt that it had gone too far, that the children were being exploited and that their duty was to disrupt the play and firmly offer alternatives. How would you have contributed to this discussion and what actions would you have taken in practice? Think about responding to this question using some of the key terminology from the ideas of Bourdieu.

## What is Postman's contribution to the debate?

Let us now consider a third useful lens – the writing of Neil Postman (1931–2003). Postman was a professor of education at New York University. He was the author of many books including one entitled *Amusing Ourselves to Death: Public Discourse in the Age of Show Business* (1985). This was an important book, and it lends a further useful lens to our discussion, because it examines how American society is imprisoned by an obsession with being entertained. According to Postman's son, Andrew, who discussed this work in a newspaper article in

2017, 'the vision portrayed in the book … is one of "a technology-sedating, consumption-engorging, instant-gratifying bubble"'; he goes on to argue that in this book Postman had foreseen the circumstances that would allow Donald Trump to become the president of the United States 30 years later (Postman, 2017). He suggests that the signs were there when the book was published, with a president in power (Ronald Reagan) who was both '[a] former actor and [a] polished communicator'. Under Reagan's influence, he argues that it was at this time that the 'political discourse … was diminished to soundbites' and that 'The nation increasingly got its "serious" information not from newspapers, which demand a level of deliberation and active engagement, but from television.'

## The disappearance of childhood

But what has all this got to do with young children and their interaction with the media? They are hardly going to be engaging in political discussions, although they are situated within the macrosystem of the political landscape if we look at this situation from the perspective of Bronfenbrenner. Before *Amusing Ourselves to Death* (1985), Postman had published a book called *The Disappearance of Childhood*. In this book he argues that, historically, childhood was a time in which the information that children had access to was controlled by adults, who decided the stages of when, where and how they got access to new information, and thus children's access to information was managed and presented in a sequential and ordered way. However, the invention of the telegraph changed that, as it shifted the speed at which information could be sent and received. This, according to Postman, 'began the process of wrestling control of information from the home and school' and 'altered the kind of information children could have access to, its quality and quantity, its sequence, and the circumstances in which it would be experienced' (1994, p. 72). In a world where everyone can access the same information at the same time, children's access to information is no longer managed and no longer able to be presented in a sequential way.

Instead, adults and children alike can have access to the same information simultaneously. Thus, 'electric media find it impossible to withhold any secrets. Without secrets, of course, there can be no such thing as childhood' (ibid.). Spend a moment taking this in. Do you think that the concept of childhood is dependent on children's managed access to information? Postman talks of television usage in particular, arguing that

> television erodes the dividing line between childhood and adulthood in 3 ways, all having to do with its undifferentiated accessibility: first, because it requires no instruction to grasp its form; second, because it does not make complex demands on either mind or behaviour; and third, because it does not segregate its audience.
>
> (1994, p. 80).

Part of this statement, the claim that television doesn't make complex demands, fits with Shin's mental effort/passivity hypothesis (2004) that we discussed in Chapter 3 (*Children's media as education, not entertainment*).

However not everyone agrees with Postman's 'disappearance of childhood' argument and that an increase in the amount of information children have access to is leading to its end. The United Nation's Convention on the Rights of the Child suggests that in fact children's access to information is protecting childhoods. The UNCRC, written in 1989 and ratified in the UK in 1991, comprises 54 rights for children worldwide. Our interest here is in Article 17 which states:

> Children have the right to get information that is important to their health and well-being. Governments should encourage mass media – radio, television, newspapers and Internet content sources – to provide information that children can understand and to not promote materials that could harm children. Mass media should particularly be encouraged to supply information in languages that minority and indigenous children can understand. Children should also have access to children's books.

This suggests that an important right in childhood is the right to information and that this access to information is a positive thing rather than something which harms children and promotes the demise of childhood. One argument around protecting children's innocence can be critiqued by others which propose the dangers of shielding children from information under the guise of preserving their innocence. For instance, viewing children as innocent in the South African context impacts on the information they are given regarding young children's right to HIV and AIDS education, which could have grave implications (Bhana, 2007). Therefore, Postman's argument that an increase in the amount of information that children have access to will erode their childhood is at odds with the UNCRC, which instead argues that ensuring children have access to relevant information is in fact protecting their childhoods.

## Time to consider

Imagine you are taking part in a debate entitled 'Media is robbing children of their childhood'. Decide if you want to argue in favour or against the statement and then list the key points that would comprise your argument. It doesn't matter whether you are for or against in reality, the idea is to build a strong argument. In fact, it is often beneficial to think about the view that opposes your own because then you begin to consider other aspects of the argument that you may have ignored otherwise. Don't worry about making your tone too assertive or whether your points lack nuance; remember they are strategic points that are developing an argument. The idea is to adopt one perspective and imagine you are trying to persuade someone who holds the opposite view. Make your argument stronger by finding relevant research to support the points you want to make.

## Final reflection

In this chapter we have remembered the importance of using a theoretical lens to help us examine more deeply issues impacting children; we have looked in particular here at how such lenses can help us understand the impact of the media in young children's lives. The three key theorists we have discussed here are Bronfenbrenner, Bourdieu and Postman. Bronfenbrenner's ecological model not only helps us consider the exosystem of the media in young children's lives, but it also supports an understanding of what the media means in the context of the child's microsystem (e.g. their family television viewing), mesosystem (e.g. whether their early years setting values the same or different media sources compared to their home setting), or their macrosystem (e.g. where they live geographically). Bourdieu has helped us understand that children's access to, consumption of, and portrayal in the media is linked to notions of their habitus (e.g. do they watch *Love Island*?) and field (do they talk about *Love Island* when they attend their ECEC setting?). We also considered his ideas around economic capital (what access does the child have to media technology?), cultural capital (can the child join in with the class discussion of *The Lego Movie* and visiting Legoland?), and social capital (are there other children in their class who they discuss their viewing habits with – or does no one else watch *Love Island*?).

## Key points

- Children's engagement with media needs to be understood according to the different contexts they find themselves in. This may be the context of the home, the ECEC setting, their ethnicity or their geographical location. It is also important to understand the interactions between these different contexts.
- Children are socialised in certain ways in these various contexts; they intuitively learn the unspoken rules of each context and adjust their behaviours and practices accordingly. They also learn rules about power relationships within these contexts.
- Theoretical thinking about children's engagement with media echoes the binary media portrayal of children. On the one hand they can be seen as robbed of their innocence and robbed of their childhood. Conversely they can be understood as informed and equipped by their engagement with the key, and easily accessible, information that the media can provide them with

## Further reading

1. Jordan, A. (2004) 'The Role of Media in Children's Development: An Ecological Perspective', *Journal of Developmental and Behavioral Pediatrics*, 25(3),

pp. 196–206. In this article Amy Jordan draws on the work of Bronfenbrenner to discuss why an ecological approach is a helpful way to consider the impact of the media on children's development.

2. McTavish, A. (n.d.) 'Cultural Capital'. Available at: www.early-education.org.uk/cultural-capital (accessed 24 August 2021). This is a great article on the Early Education website that not only considers the term 'cultural capital' in the context of early childhood, but also what it could look like in practice.
3. Postman, A. (2017) 'My Dad Predicted Trump in 1985 – It's Not Orwell, He Warned, It's Brave New World'. Available at: www.theguardian.com/media/2017/feb/02/amusing-ourselves-to-death-neil-postman-trump-orwell-huxley (accessed 26 August 2021). This is a great newspaper article which will really get you thinking. It is written by Neil Postman's son; he sets out an argument about the negative impact of the media age and how we have become imprisoned by an obsession with being entertained.

## References

Alanen, L., Brooker, E. and Mayall, B. (2015) *Childhood with Bourdieu*. Basingstoke: Palgrave Macmillan.

Bhana, D. (2007) 'The Price of Innocence: Teachers, Gender, Childhood Sexuality, HIV and AIDS in Early Schooling', *International Journal of Inclusive Education*, 11(4), pp. 431–444.

Bolshaw, P. and Josephidou, J. (2018) *Introducing Research in Early Childhood*. London: Sage.

Bourdieu, P. (2000) 'The Politics of Protest: An Interview with K. Ovenden', *Socialist Review*, 242, pp. 18–20.

Bourdieu, P. and Wacquant, L. (1992) *An Invitation to Reflexive Sociology*. Chicago: Chicago University Press.

Bronfenbrenner, U. (1994) 'Ecological Models of Human Development', In U. Bronfenbrenner, *Readings on the Development of Children*, 2nd ed. New York: Freeman, pp. 37–43.

Bronfenbrenner, U. and Ceci, S.J. (1994) 'Nature-Nurture Reconceptualised: A Bio-Ecological Model', *Psychological Review*, 10(4), pp. 568–586.

Convention on the Rights of the Child (1989) Treaty no. 27541. *United Nations Convention on the Rights of the Child*, 1577: 4–14. Available at: https://downloads.unicef.org.uk/wp-content/uploads/2010/05/UNCRC_united_nations_convention_on_the_rights_of_the_child.pdf?_ga=2.119561160.1753319808.1496413662-596175726.1496413662 (accessed 7 July 2021).

Davies, L. (2014) 'Working Positively with the Media to Protect Children', *Journal of Social Welfare and Family Law*, 36(1), pp. 47–58.

Jago, R., Stamatakis, E., Gama, A., Carvalhal, I.M., Nogueira, H., Rosado, V. and Padez, C. (2012) 'Parent and Child Screen-Viewing Time and Home Media Environment', *American Journal of Preventive Medicine*, 43(2), pp. 150–158.

Jordan, A. (2004) 'The Role of Media in Children's Development: An Ecological Perspective', *Journal of Developmental and Behavioral Pediatrics*, 25(3), pp. 196–206.

Jordan, A. (2005) 'Learning to Use Books and Television – An Exploratory Study in the Ecological Perspective', *American Behavioral Scientist*, 48(5), pp. 523–538.

Lang, S. (2005) *Urie Bronfenbrenner, father of Head Start program and pre-eminent 'human ecologist,' dies at age 88*. Available at: https://news.cornell.edu/stories/2005/09/head-start-founder-urie-bronfenbrenner-dies-88 (accessed 21 August 2021).

Lynskey, D. (2014) 'Frozen-Mania: How Elsa, Anna and Olaf Conquered the World'. Available at: www.theguardian.com/film/2014/may/13/frozen-mania-elsa-anna-olaf-disney-emo-princess-let-it-go (accessed 26 August 2021).

Ofsted (2019) 'Early Years Inspection Handbook'. Available at: https://assets.publishing.service.gov.uk/government/uploads/system/uploads/attachment_data/file/801599/Early_years_inspection_draft_handbook_140119_archived.pdf (accessed 11 September 2021).

Palmer, S. (2019) Defining 'cultural capital' in terms of best practice. Available at: www-magonlinelibrary-com.libezproxy.open.ac.uk/doi/full/10.12968/eyed.2019.21.2.14 (accessed 11 September 2021).

Pires, P., Ribas, R. and Borzekowski, D. (2015) 'Attitudes and Intentions to Smoke: A Study of Young Brazilian Children', *Child: Care, Health and Development*, 41(6), pp. 1124–1130.

Postman, A. (2017) 'My Dad Predicted Trump in 1985 – It's Not Orwell, He Warned, It's Brave New World'. Available at: www.theguardian.com/media/2017/feb/02/amusing-ourselves-to-death-neil-postman-trump-orwell-huxley (accessed 26 August 2021).

Postman, N. (1982) *The Disappearance of Childhood*. New York: Vintage Books.

Postman, N. (1985) *Amusing Ourselves to Death: Public Discourse in the Age of Show Business*. New York: Penguin Books.

Postman, N. (1994) *The Disappearance of Childhood*. New York: Vintage Books.

Rosa, E. and Tudge, J. (2013) 'Urie Bronfenbrenner's Theory of Human Development: Its Evolution from Ecology to Bioecology', *Journal of Family Theory & Review*, 5, pp. 243–258.

Selwyn, N., Bananji, S., Hadjithoma-Garstka, C. and Clark, W. (2011) 'Providing a Platform for Parents? Exploring the Nature of Parental Engagement with School Learning Platform', *Journal of Computer Assisted Learning*, 27, pp. 314–323.

Shin, N. (2004) 'Exploring Pathways from Television Viewing to Academic Achievement in School Age Children', *The Journal of Genetic Psychology*, 165(4), pp. 367–382.

Tudge, J., Navarro, J., Merçon-Vargas, E. and Payir, A. (2021) 'The Promise and the Practice of Early Childhood Educare in the Writings of Urie Bronfenbrenner', *Early Child Development and Care*, 191(7–8), pp. 1079–1088.

The Vocabularist (2016) 'When Is a Theory "Just a Theory"'? Available at: www.bbc.co.uk/news/blogs-magazine-monitor-35499049 (accessed 25 August 2021).

Vuorisalo, M. and Alanen, L. (2015) 'Early Childhood Education as a Social Field', in L. Alanen, E. Brooker and B. Mayall (eds), *Childhood with Bourdieu*. Basingstoke: Palgrave Macmillan, pp. 78–98.

PART

III

# How can we minimise the risks of children's media use?

CHAPTER

# 9 Born digital

## Promoting young children's media literacy

## Introduction

Do you remember becoming literate? Can you recall the process of learning the different sounds that individual letters make, how these individual letters came together to make words, and then how sentences were constructed? Some children pick up reading very easily, whereas for others it is a painstaking process. But in the twenty-first century, being literate is not merely about being able to read and write. Kerry-Moran (2021) draws on others' research to argue that to be literate today means to be able to 'encode and decode across a multiplicity of sociocultural contexts and sign systems' (p. 37); she argues that, whereas at one time the printed word encapsulated the term 'literacy', this is no longer the case, with multimodal literacies such as those of image and sound coming to the fore.

Ten years before Kerry-Moran was writing, Professor Renee Hobbs, an internationally-recognised authority on digital and media literacy education, acknowledged this need to be literate in twenty-first-century terms. In her White Paper (2010), entitled 'Digital and Media Literacy: A Plan of Action', she reminds the reader that definitions of literacy are fluid and that 'the concept of literacy is beginning to be defined as the ability to share meaning through symbol systems in order to fully participate in society … [these] symbol systems, include[e] language, still and moving images, graphic design, sound, music and interactivity' (pp. 17–18). At the same time, she stresses the importance of being able to 'access, analyze [sic] and engage in critical thinking' about these systems (p. vii). This argument contrasts with everyday perceptions of media engagement as a low-level skill that does not need to be taught; children just 'do it', i.e. engage with media. Think of the clichéd scenario of a parent using the television as a 'babysitter', or watch a 2 year old intuitively swiping a mobile phone or a tablet.

Parents of course can choose to regulate what children can watch on TV or they can monitor their child's use of the internet; but how many parents teach their children how to engage with these sources in the critical way that Hobbs (2010) emphasises? Schools teach internet safety, through a variety of curricu-

DOI: 10.4324/9781003121206-12

lum areas such as Relationships Education, Health Education and Citizenship Education (DfE, 2019), but do they teach children how adverts can manipulate, the hidden messages of a Disney film or who is missing from the media they engage with? We are a global society that places a high value on literacy, so that 'In many countries, even relatively low levels of basic skills in numeracy and literacy attract a wage premium' (Cherry and Vignoles, 2020), yet do we teach children from a young age how to be both digitally and media literate? These are some of the questions we intend to explore in this chapter. We hope that by the end of this chapter, not only will you have an enhanced understanding of what it means to be both media and digitally literate in the twenty-first century, but you will also know how to support these important skills in young children. In addition, if you are working with families and communities, you will have a developed understanding of different resources you can use to work with them.

## What is digital literacy and what is media literacy?

### Digital literacy

A useful source for definitions around the topic of digital literacy is JISC (Joint Information Systems Committee). This organisation works with universities to support young people with their digital engagement. JISC define digital literacies as 'capabilities … for living, learning and working in a digital society', and they outline seven key elements, as can be seen in Table 9.1. The first column sets out the seven elements, while the middle column gives JISC's explanation of what this looks like in practice. However, you will note that some of this terminology is not appropriate for young children; yet we do not want them to wait until they are young adults to begin to acquire these important skills; therefore, in the final column, we have suggested what these elements could look like within the ECEC setting.

JISC suggest that digital literacy is a developmental model; they use Beetham and Sharpe's framework (2010) to demonstrate this progression (see Figure 9.1).

### Media literacy

JISC's (2014) definitions of digital literacies that we have outlined above appear to be thorough and detailed, so what can the term 'media literacy' contribute that adds to our understanding of the key skills needed to navigate our way through a digital society? It is true to say that there is an overlap in the research literature when the two areas (i.e. digital literacy and media literacy) are discussed; however it is useful here to explore in a little more detail how various sources discuss and define this latter term.

**TABLE 9.1** The seven elements of digital literacies (adapted from JISC, 2014)

| The seven elements | JISC's description of what this looks like in practice | Our interpretation of what this could look like in ECEC |
|---|---|---|
| *Media literacy* | Critically read and creatively produce academic and professional communication in a range of media | Critically interpret, read, and produce communication in a range of (developmentally appropriate) media |
| *Communication and collaboration* | Participate in digital networks for learning and research | Participate and collaborate with peers through digital means as part of holistic development |
| *Career and identity management* | Manage digital reputation and online identity | Develop an understanding (developmentally appropriate) of not sharing personal information online |
| *ICT literacy* | Adopt, adapt and use digital devices, applications and services | Adopt, adapt and use digital devices, applications and services in a developmentally appropriate manner |
| *Learning skills* | Study and learn effectively in technology-rich environments, formal and informal | Develop and learn effectively in technology-rich enabling environments |
| *Digital scholarship* | Participate in emerging academic, professional and research practices that depend on digital systems | Develop age-appropriate research skills and share findings with peers |
| *Information literacy* | Find, interpret, evaluate, manage and share information | Find, interpret, evaluate, manage and share information in developmentally appropriate ways |

**FIGURE 9.1** A pyramid model of digital literacy (adapted from Beetham and Sharpe (2010), cited by JISC, 2014)

Media literacy can be seen as 'a subset of multiliteracy', in the words of Burn and Durran (2007, p. 4). Then, under the umbrella term of media literacy, they set out further subsets, including:

- moving image literacy
- cine-literacy
- television literacy
- game literacy

They advise that 'learning *about* the media' should not become mistaken for 'learning *through* the media', and they draw on the work of Ofcom, and the responsibilities it has for ensuring that media literacy skills are developed, noting in particular their definition of media literacy as being able to access the media, understand the media and create media (Ofcom, n.d.). Livingstone notes 'the imperative ... to identify, and to manage the development of skills and abilities required' (2003, p. 3). She adds further forms of literacy to the list, including:

- computer literacy
- internet literacy
- cyber-literacy

Her definition of media literacy is 'the ability to access, analyse, evaluate and create messages across a variety of contexts' (ibid.).

Legislation (The Communications Act 2003) requires media literacy to be promoted and researched. This task falls to Ofcom (The Office of Communications), who produce regular reports about this work. The 2016 report focused on children aged 3 to 15 and the views of their parents. One of their interesting findings was that children's effective application of media skills depended on the digital context; they 'were more likely to apply [these] ... for instance for homework or important information, rather than just entertainment' (p. 8).

## Differences between digital literacy and media literacy

We have considered in isolation these two forms of literacy, but what is their relationship to each other? There is some overlap between the two concepts as they both require children to engage with critical thinking; the relationship between the two ideas is explained by MediaSmarts (n.d.) who suggest that 'media literacy generally focuses on teaching youth to be critically engaged consumers of media, while digital literacy is more about enabling youth to participate in digital media in wise, safe and ethical ways'. They also explain that these two areas of literacy do not 'run parallel' to each other but rather that digital literacy 'builds on' media literacy and, conversely, that 'many digital issues cannot be understood without traditional media literacy' (ibid.). This is clarified further in Table 9.2 which sets out two examples of the underpinning of digital literacy by media literacy.

## Time to consider

Consider the specific forms of media literacy referenced by Burn and Durran (2007, p. 4) (moving image literacy, cine-literacy, television literacy, and game literacy). Now consider:

- examples of these kinds of literacy for young children
- the knowledge and understanding needed to engage with this kind of literacy
- how an adult could support children in developing this knowledge and understanding
- why it is important

When you have thought through some of these ideas, have a go at completing Table 9.3. We have added some ideas to prompt your thinking.

**TABLE 9.2** The link between media literacy and digital literacy (adapted from MediaSmarts, n.d.)

| Media literacy | Digital literacy |
|---|---|
| Explore the commercial considerations of online services | Understand why online services want to collect their personal information |
| Recognise that algorithms (such as Google's search algorithm or Facebook's News Feed) are made by people and that they are not neutral tools but rather reflect the biases and assumptions of their creators | Understand the role of algorithms (such as Google's search algorithm or Facebook's News Feed) in shaping our online experience and behaviour |

**TABLE 9.3** Strategies to develop knowledge, understanding and skills for specific media literacy sources

| Specific literacy type | Example | Knowledge, understanding and skills needed | Why this knowledge, understanding and these skills are important | Strategies to develop knowledge, understanding and skills |
|---|---|---|---|---|
| *Moving image* | *Peppa Pig* | | | |
| *Cine-literacy* | *Encanto* | | | |
| *Television literacy* | *I'm a Celebrity ... Get Me Out of Here*[*] | | | |
| *Game literacy* | *Animal Crossing for Nintendo Switch* | | | |

[*] This an adult programme (i.e. after the watershed), however there is evidence that it has a substantial child audience: 'the top viewed programme by children aged 4–15 ... in Wales and Northern Ireland ... was I'm a Celebrity ... Get me out of here!' (Ofcom, 2021).

## Why are digital literacy and media literacy important?

In the previous section we considered different ways that digital literacy and media literacy can be defined. Now we are going to look more closely at the importance of developing the associated skills.

### Multimodal textual landscapes

Let us return here to Kerry-Moran's definition (2021) of what it means to be literate in the twenty-first century, i.e. to be able to 'encode and decode across a multiplicity of sociocultural contexts and sign systems' (p. 37). What do these contexts and systems look like in everyday life? 'Multimodal textual landscape' is a term used by Carrington and Robinson (2011) to describe the context of an individual engaging with the world outside their home. Although they are describing the context in Hong Kong, their description could easily fit any other big city in the world. In the introduction to their book *Digital Literacies: Social Learning and Classroom Practices* (2011), Carrington and Robinson depict a scene which perfectly illustrates the importance of digital and media literacy:

> We are surrounded by texts … Some texts are printed, some are digital, some are permanent, while others are ephemeral … Laminated food menus throughout the city mix and match photographs with Cantonese and imaginative English translations. Marketing staff hand out flyers and tissues on every street corner; screens run the length of skyscrapers and move restlessly from advertising to news and weather and back again; every bar and every subway train has multiple screens playing news and different sporting events. At the same time, kerbside stands are bursting with printed newspapers, magazines and graphic novels, while graffiti and stickering … provide a parallel discourse on the city that adds to the cacophony of text. No one form of text reigns supreme; together they construct the **multimodal textual landscape** of the city.
>
> (p. 1)

### Within the ECEC setting

We can imagine a young child in the context of this busy city street scene, engaging with all these different systems. They reach the end of the street and enter the ECEC setting; a different context with different digital systems to engage in. They pick up a tablet and begin their play and learning. Wohlwend (2015) examined this digital play; in particular she observed children collaboratively using an app to create a story. She compared this activity, 'with many hands all busy dragging, resizing, and animating puppet characters, and many voices making sound effects, narrating, directing, and objecting', with 'the orderly matching activities in prevalent letter and word recognition apps that dominate early childhood educational software' (p. 154). She suggests that, regardless of the noise and apparent chaos, there is a complexity to the children's play as they engage in 'coordinated storying, digital literacy learning, multimodal production, and play negotiation' (p. 154). These young children are demonstrating the fact that, 'In the early 21st century, definitions of literacy have evolved to include multiple ways of working with a variety of screen-based media, including web pages, videos, video games, and apps on mobile devices' (p. 157).

### Time to consider

In Wohlwend's (2015) article, she considers the vast range of electronic technology that children have access to, in the home, in the ECEC setting and in school. You could begin by listing the technology you have seen children interacting with in these contexts. Now think of some ways that children could be supported to evaluate the information that they access on these devices. What about creation of their own content? How could children be given opportunities in early years settings to create their own online media? You may be able to recall examples of this that you have observed in the setting. How would you evaluate these opportunities? For example, did you note the same complex collaborative work that Wohlwend (2015) suggests. If not, why was this?

## How can we foster digital literacy and media literacy?

There are very many resources online to foster both digital literacy and media literacy, although, ironically, we could argue that digitally fluent adults are required to be able to critique them before they can be offered to children as useful tools.

One such useful webpage belongs to MediaSmart who offer resources for parents and teachers of children aged from 7 upwards to enable them to develop the 'understanding and tools they need to be critical consumers of the media' (n.d.). The organisation cites the key skills of media literacy as 'resilience, empathy, creativity, communication and critical-thinking' (ibid.); these are without doubt all important life skills for young children's holistic development.

The *Growing Up Digital* report by the Children's Commissioner (2017) remarks that although 'The internet is an extraordinary force for good', nevertheless 'it is not designed with children in mind' (p. 3). At the same time, it recognises the great number of children who use the internet (i.e. one-third of its users) and the increasing amount of time they spend doing this (e.g. for 3-4 year olds in 2016 it was 8 hours 18 minutes per week). Because of this fact, the report asserts that 'much more needs to be done to create a supportive digital environment for children and young people' (ibid.), calling for three interventions from the government. These interventions are:

1. A digital citizenship programme for children from 4 to 14
2. Simplified T&C for digital services offered to children
3. A new Children's Digital Ombudsman

## Digital resilience

Resilience is a key idea in terms of the skills children need in their engagement with the media. Zolkoski and Bullock (2012) suggest that 'resilience require(s) conditions of an identified risk or challenge followed by some defined measure of positive outcome' (p. 2296). They continue, 'debate remains concerning what constitutes resilient behavior and how to best measure successful adaptation to hardship' (ibid.). Most importantly, they argue that this is not a skill or disposition that you either have or do not have; rather it can be developed. In this section we are interested to understand what resilience means in terms of children's digital engagement, and how we can help them develop this kind of resilience.

The role of the adult is key in supporting children to develop the appropriate resilience to be able to engage digitally. EU Kids Online (2014) recommends that parents in particular should 'Focus on enhancing children's opportunities, coping skills and resilience to potential harm' (p. 35). Findings from a variety of research projects this organisation has engaged in really stress the benefits of online engagement and how this links to risk. For example, they suggest:

- The more children use the internet, the more digital skills they gain, and the higher they climb the 'ladder of online opportunities' to gain the benefits.
- Not all internet use results in benefits: the chance of a child gaining the benefits depends on their age, gender and socio-economic status, on how their parents support them, and on the positive content available to them.
- Children's use, skills and opportunities are also linked to online risks; the more of these, the more risk of harm; thus, as internet use increases, ever greater efforts are needed to prevent risk also increasing.

(p. 9)

However, parents also need to be both resilient and confident to most effectively support children in this way. Yet they do not always display this confidence and their fears do not always align with the understanding that the children have. If we look at the Children's Commissioner's report (2017, p. 4), we can see this fact illustrated in her comment that there is 'A mismatch of knowledge, fears and expectations between parents and their children'. This statement also echoes findings from EU Kids Online (2014) who found that 'Parents see online risks as being from strangers, whereas children see the risks as coming from people they know.' Of course, there are other key adults in children's lives beside their parents; yet these other adults may lack the knowhow to support children in developing resilience. For example, in data drawn from a survey which involved senior leaders, staff, governors and staff across 39 primary schools and 45 secondary schools, as part of the inspection process, Ofsted (2015) found that although '59% of staff "strongly agree" and 28% "agree" that they've had effective training in online safety issues in the last 12 months ... training can be inconsistent, and what senior leaders see as training might not be reflected by staff'. This situation means that many teachers (to be precise, 38% of Ofsted's sample) do not feel sufficiently able to manage any issues to do with children's online engagement.

Ofsted's findings are noteworthy if we consider the findings from a published report (NSPCC, 2016) the following year. This report found that 'The number of children contacting Childline about cyberbullying ... increased by 88% in 5 years.' This included children as young as 7 years old and included comments about children's appearance, death threats and even encouragement to kill themselves. If we jump ahead five years from this NSPCC report to 2021, we learn that Zhu et al.'s research (2021) finds that cyberbullying has become a 'serious public health issue' (p. 1) because of its impact on children's mental health. However, if we return to the idea of resilience, we find that this piece of research concludes that 'possible strategies for cyberbullying prevention ... [are] ... personal emotion management, digital ability training, policy applicability, interpersonal skills', whilst at the same time acknowledging the role of the parent in supporting these strategies (p. 10).

To conclude this section, what is of key importance in supporting children in developing the appropriate digital skills is the idea of developing 'digital resilience'. In the context of children's online engagement, this could mean how, in the face of risk offered by online engagement, we can ensure that children experience positive outcomes. We have seen that a key role of parents, carers and those that work with young children is to ensure that we help them develop this resilience. Yet we have also seen through the Ofsted survey that not all adults feel confident in being able to do this, so that there is a need not just to digitally educate children but also to digitally educate those adults who care for them. This is particularly important in the context of cyberbullying and giving children the appropriate skills and knowledge to know how to deal with this.

## Digital literacy, media literacy and children's rights

It is helpful to consider digital and media literacy within the context of children's rights. In fact children themselves have made the link between their rights and their interaction with digital media, according to Livingstone (2016).

She summarises their views in the four points below:

1. The internet and mobile technologies are becoming a key means by which children exercise their rights to information, education and participation.
2. Consequently, access to the internet and mobile technologies must also be a basic right.
3. Since access is insufficient without media or digital literacy, that too is now fundamental to exercising rights in a digital age.
4. Children expect their voices to be heard in formal and informal processes of deliberation wherever their rights in a digital age are at stake.

(pp. 2–3)

One initiative, developed by various organisations such as the NSPCC, NASUWT (a teaching union) and Mozilla (a free software community), has looked to interpret children's digital rights and therefore produced 'The 5Rights' framework (5rights, n.d.). This sets out ways that children can be protected and empowered in their interactions with the digital world, and it is informed by the United Nations Convention on the Rights of the Child. The five rights of the framework are:

- The right to know
- The right to remove
- The right to safety and support
- The right to informed and conscious use
- The right to digital literacy

In their document 'Enabling Children and Young People to Access the Digital World Creatively, Knowledgeably and Fearlessly' (iRights, 2015), they acknowledge that 'The internet and digital technologies have created vast opportunities for children and young people to learn, to communicate and to explore', but that the best way to enable children to fully benefit from these opportunities was to prepare them fully by acknowledging these rights.

Others have considered young children's digital rights within the context of Article 31.1 ('The right of the child to rest and leisure, to engage in play and recreational activities appropriate to the age of the child and to participate freely in cultural life and the arts' (UNHCR, 1989). For example, Jørgensen and Skovbjerg (2021) considered the idea of media literacy along play which includes computer games. They carried out research with children who were aged 5 and 6 within the context of ECEC settings in Denmark. They found that having asked children to make drawings and chat about their favourite computer games, some reported great excitement about the game *Grand Theft Auto*. This was surprising as it is a game rated 18+ because of violent content. As the researcher probed

**TABLE 9.4** Identified risks and challenges, strategies, and positive outcomes

| Specific literacy type | Example | Identified risks and challenges | Strategies | Positive outcomes |
|---|---|---|---|---|
| *Moving image* | *Peppa Pig* | Child would spend too long passively watching TV | ■ Adult takes time to watch with child so that there is rich discussion<br>■ Adult and child agree/negotiate frequency and duration of screen time | Child takes lead in following agreed 'rules' around screen time |
| *Cine-literacy* | *Encanto* | | | |
| *Television literacy* | *I'm a Celebrity ... Get Me Out of Here* | | | |
| *Game literacy* | *Animal Crossing* for Nintendo Switch | | | |

with further questions, it became apparent that these children had not necessarily played *Grand Theft Auto*; their interest in the game appeared to come from older siblings' or parents' engagement with it. At face value, it could be worrying that young children were fascinated by inappropriate and violent content; however it becomes clear that the children interpret this prohibited software as representing 'the fascination and fun of crashing and turning the world upside down', which Jørgensen and Skovbjerg link to the 'silliness, nonsense and wildness of play' (2021, p. 157).

## Time to consider

Zolkoski and Bullock (2012) suggest that 'resilience require(s) conditions of an identified risk or challenge followed by some defined measure of positive outcome' (p. 2296). Go back to the first 'Time to consider' activity in this chapter (see Table 9.3) and recall the sources you thought about then. This time, for each source, what risks and challenges would you identify, what strategies could be put in place to deal with these, and what would you consider to be a measure of a defined outcome? It may help to fill in a table as shown in Table 9.4.

## Final reflection

In this chapter we have considered what is meant by the terms 'media literacy' and 'digital literacy', and how they are defined by different writers. We have also considered why it is so important to support young children to develop these kinds of literacy skills in an ever changing world.

There are many useful sources we can seek out to find out about strategies to promote this type of literacy and we have considered some of these. Before you go on to the next chapter, take some time to reflect on the following points:

- What do you now understand by 'media literacy' and 'digital literacy'?
- How can we foster children with digital resilience, digital information, and who have digital power?
- How can we critique proposed interventions?

## Key points

- Children are growing up in a global society which has much broader definitions of literacy than those of previous generations; these multiliteracies include such subsets as computer literacy; internet literacy; cyber-literacy; moving image literacy; cine-literacy; television literacy; game literacy.
- Any negative impact of the digital world can be addressed by teaching children strategies to navigate these multimodal textual landscapes, whether that be at a macro, meso or micro level. These strategies can not only reduce the negative impact, but they can also ensure that children get the most benefit from these forms of literacy.
- Children can be taught to become critical consumers of the digital world, consumers who are informed, safe and resilient.

## Further reading

1. Burn, A. and Durran, J. (2007) *Media Literacy in Schools: Practice, Production and Progression*. London: Paul Chapman Publishing.Although this book is over ten years old, it is a useful resource. It includes useful case studies and links media literacy to issues of self-esteem. Read in particular chapter 1: 'What is Media Literacy?' (pages 1–22).
2. MediaSmarts (n.d.) Available at: https://mediasmarts.ca/digital-media-literacy/general-information/digital-media-literacy-fundamentals/intersection-digital-media-lieracy (accessed 27 August 2021).MediaSmarts is a Canadian charity which promotes digital and media literacy. Its website is a wonderful source of information and resources, both for practitioners and parents.

3. Hobbs, R. (2010) *Digital and Media Literacy: A Plan of Action.* Available at: https://files.eric.ed.gov/fulltext/ED523244.pdf (accessed 13 August 2021). This report is a great read, although it is now over ten years old. It sets out how to incorporate digital and media literacy skills into people's (including children's) everyday lives.

## References

Burn, A. and Durran, J. (2007) *Media Literacy in Schools: Practice, Production and Progression.* London: Paul Chapman Publishing.

Carrington, V. and Robinson, M. (2011) *Digital Literacies: Social Learning and Classroom Practices.* London: Sage.

Cherry, G. and Vignoles, A. (2020) *What Is the Economic Value of Literacy and Numeracy?* Available at: https://wol.iza.org/articles/what-is-economic-value-of-literacy-and-numeracy/long (accessed 29 August 2021).

Children's Commissioner (2017) *Growing Up Digital: A Report of the Growing Up Digital Taskforce.* Available at: www.childrenscommissioner.gov.uk/wp-content/uploads/2017/06/Growing-Up-Digital-Taskforce-Report-January-2017_0.pdf (accessed 29 August 2021).

DfE (Department for Education) (2019) *Teaching online safety in school: Guidance supporting schools to teach their pupils how to stay safe online, within new and existing school subjects.* Available at: https://assets.publishing.service.gov.uk/government/uploads/system/uploads/attachment_data/file/811796/Teaching_online_safety_in_school.pdf (accessed 29 August 2021).

EU Kids Online (2014) *Findings, Methods and Recommendations.* Available at: http://eprints.lse.ac.uk/60512/1/EU%20Kids%20onlinie%20III%20.pdf (accessed 29 August 2021).

5rights (n.d.) 'The 5rights'. Available from: https://5rightsframework.com/the-5-rights/ (accessed 30 August 2021).

Hobbs, R. (2010) *Digital and Media Literacy: A Plan of Action.* Available at: https://files.eric.ed.gov/fulltext/ED523244.pdf (accessed 13 August 2021).

iRights (2015) 'Enabling Children and Young People to Access the Digital World. Creatively, Knowledgeably and Fearlessly'. Available at: www.itu.int/en/council/cwg-cop/Documents/iRights%20Full%20Text%20Revised%20Sept%202015%20.pdf (accessed 29 August 2021).

JISC (Joint Information Systems Committee) (2014) *Developing Digital Literacies.* Available at: www.jisc.ac.uk/guides/developing-digital-literacies (accessed 27 August 2021)

Jørgensen, H. and Skovbjerg, H. (2021) 'Understanding the Mutuality of Play and Media Literacy in Young Children', in D. Holloway, M. Willson, K. Murcia, C. Archer and F. Stocco (eds), *Young Children's Rights in a Digital World.* Cham, Switzerland: Springer, pp. 147–159.

Kerry-Moran, K. (2021) 'A Dilemma for the Teacher Educator: Navigating the 21st Century Literacy Landscape', in M. Narey and K. Kerry-Moran (eds), *Sense-Making: Problematizing Constructs of Literacy for 21st Century Education.* Cham, Switzerland: Springer, pp. 37–53.

Livingstone, S. (2003) *The Changing Nature and Uses of Media Literacy.* Available at: http://eprints.lse.ac.uk/13476/1/The_changing_nature_and_uses_of_media_literacy.pdf (accessed 28 August 2021).

Livingstone, S. (2016) *Children's rights in the digital age.* Available at: http://eprints.lse.ac.uk/67341/1/Livingstone_Childrens_rights_digital_age_author.pdf (accessed 30 August 2021).

MediaSmart (n.d.) *About us.* Available at: https://mediasmart.uk.com/about-us/ (accessed 29 August 2021).

MediaSmarts (n.d.) *The Intersection of Digital and Media Literacy.* Available at: https://mediasmarts.ca/digital-media-literacy/general-information/digital-media-literacy-fundamentals/intersection-digital-media-literacy (accessed 28 August 2021).

NSPCC (2016) *88% rise in Childline counselling sessions about cyberbullying.* Available at: www.nspcc.org.uk/fighting-for-childhood/news-opinion/88-rise-childline-counselling-sessions-cyberbullying/ (accessed 29 December 2021).

Ofcom (Office of Communications) (n.d.) *About media literacy.* Available at: www.ofcom.org.uk/research-and-data/media-literacy-research/media-literacy (accessed 30 August 2021).

Ofcom (Office of Communications) (2016) *Children and Parents: Media Use Attitudes Report.* Available at: https://www.ofcom.org.uk/__data/assets/pdf_file/0034/93976/Children-Parents-Media-Use-Attitudes-Report-2016.pdf.

Ofcom (2021) *Children and Parents: Media Use and Attitudes Report 2020/2021.* Available at: www.ofcom.org.uk/__data/assets/pdf_file/0025/217825/children-and-parents-media-use-and-attitudes-report-2020-21.pdf (accessed 8 September 2021).

Ofsted (2015) *Child Internet Safety Summit: Online Safety and Inspection.* Available at: www.slideshare.net/Ofstednews/childinternetsafetysummitonlinesafetyinspection (accessed 29 August 2021).

UNHCR (1989). *Convention on the Rights of the Child.* Available from: www.ohchr.org/en/professionalinterest/pages/crc.aspx. (accessed 30 August 2021).

Wohlwend, K.E. (2015) 'One Screen, Many Fingers: Young Children's Collaborative Literacy Play with Digital Puppetry Apps and Touchscreen Technologies', *Theory into Practice*, 52(2), pp. 154–162.

Zhu, C., Huang, S., Evans, R. and Zhang, W. (2021) 'Cyberbullying among Adolescents and Children: A Comprehensive Review of the Global Situation, Risk Factors, and Preventive Measures', *Frontiers in Public Health*, 9, pp. 1–12.

Zolkoski, S.M. and Bullock, L.M. (2012) 'Resilience in Children and Youth: A Review', *Children and Youth Services Review*, 34(12), pp. 2295–2303.

CHAPTER

# 10 Children and new digital media

## The risks and the benefits

## Introduction

Type 'Best websites for children' into Google and you will receive over 8 million results. So where to start? How can the parent, carer or practitioner know which websites to completely avoid, which may be problematic, or which will be most beneficial for the children in their care? And when we use the term 'beneficial' we are not necessarily thinking about the most educational. Children's access to online games could be linked to their right to play (UNHCR, 1989), as we discussed in Chapter 9 (*Born digital: Promoting young children's media literacy*), but what criteria should we use to select the best ones? If you use a search engine to find websites for your own use, how do you filter which to rely on? Do you ask your peers to recommend? Do you trust familiar names? And do you use these same strategies when searching for appropriate websites for children? These are reasonable strategies to use in their own way, although, as we will discover in this chapter, they could also at times be problematic.

## What are the risks and benefits of children's media use and how are these portrayed?

### A selection of websites and the portrayal of good digital parents

You may recall in Chapter 7 (*Innocent, invisible or feral: Constructions of children in the media*) we considered how parents are portrayed in the media. This theme is explored further here, along with the perception that there are 'good parents' who let their children access 'good websites', as noted by Willett (2015). Let's have a look at the three websites that Willett chooses to analyse; these are *Club Penguin*, *Poptropica*, and *Minecraft*.

DOI: 10.4324/9781003121206-13

### Club Penguin

*Club Penguin* online recently made the news as visits to its website 'surged during the … pandemic with more than a million new players' (Tidy, 2020). Yet this popularity caused problems as it attracted adults who used the site to communicate inappropriately with children. As a result of this situation, Disney, the original owners but who had allowed fans to run the site since 2017, announced that legal action would be taken if the site was not closed. Previously Disney had ensured effective moderation was in place, but this appears to have been far from the case when the site was handed over. Willett is writing six years before these problems emerged; in her analysis of the website, she notes, ironically, that *Club Penguin* was seen as a 'good website' that attracted 'good parents' because the children were not exposed to advertisements on it. There appears to now be a third incarnation of *Club Penguin* called 'Club Penguin Rewritten'; its website carries the disclaimer 'Club Penguin Rewritten is a fan-made recreation of Disney's Club Penguin and is not affiliated with The Walt Disney Company and/or Disney Games and Interactive Experiences', but whether it remains any safer for children remains to be seen.

### Poptropica

Another perceived 'good website' is *Poptropica*. Here, children engage in quests and problem-solving activities. Parents encourage use of this website for their children as, in Willett's (2015) words, it 'offers parents a compromise by providing a site connected with "good" media (books), albeit in a commercial environment' (p. 1073). Pearson (n.d.) promote *Poptropica* as an educational resource that will engage 'young learners like never before', through its 'fun-filled online activities, songs and games', which create 'a world of excitement and adventure that children won't want to leave'.

### Minecraft

*Minecraft* is an exceptionally popular website with both adults and children alike. This 'building-and-exploring game … played by 90 million people every month' (Stuart, 2019) is perceived as a 'good website'. Writing as a parent, Stuart (2019) explains why:

> You don't win or lose in Minecraft. It presents you with a blocky world that you are free to explore. You chop down trees and make a house, you mine for materials, you can make a sword and fight zombies, but the fun – the reward structure – is all extrinsic: it's about exploring your own creativity, making your own rules, hanging out.

Willett echoes these ideas in her own analysis where she reflects that 'Minecraft is constructed as both independent and creative, a powerful discursive construction which trumps other concerns parents may have about their children being online' (2015, p. 1073).

Willett's analysis demonstrates that parents are portrayed as the 'evaluators, selectors, and monitors of children's online activities' (p. 1060). At the same time, by encouraging use of the three websites we have described, they understand themselves to be 'good parents' as opposed to the 'less informed and discriminating parents' (p. 1073) who are more permissive in terms of what they allow their children to access. What is most interesting about her discussion is that she believes there is a demonstration here of moral panic narratives 'drawing on hierarchies … established in relation to parenting and media since … the 1950s … [narratives that] … tap into parents' aspirations and anxieties' (ibid.).

## Media literate parents

Let's have a look at these parental fears more closely here, and in particular the fear of paedophiles accessing their children online. Media reports, such as that of Crawford (2016), set out how social platforms, and in particular Facebook, allow even convicted paedophiles to easily and anonymously share images of children through private groups with names that leave no doubt about their focus. Crawford's article accuses Facebook of 'not doing enough to police the groups and protect children', regardless of its espoused commitment to do so.

Crawford then followed up this article in 2017, further criticising Facebook for the way it handles this important issue. He cites Damian Collins (chairman of the Commons Media Committee) as having 'grave doubts' about Facebook's monitoring procedures. Crawford is inclined to agree with this statement as he reports that the BBC (his employer) had informed Facebook about a large number of inappropriate photographs on its site, but very little action had been taken; in fact, the main action was to report the BBC and its investigative journalists to the police!

Others sharing Crawford's concerns include the Children's Commissioner, Anne Longfield, whom Crawford cites in his article as being 'disturbed and disappointed' (2017) by the situation. Three years later, seeing little change, Longfield (2020) penned an open letter to Nick Clegg who was by then Head of Global Affairs at Facebook. In the letter she references an interview he gave to the BBC where he discussed 'concerns … regarding the worrying ease with which children … can access harmful, upsetting and even dangerous content'. She suggests there is some frustration with the situation on his part and that he appears to be accusing parents of lacking understanding about the difficulty of the task for such a huge social media platform. Yet she concludes: 'The scale of Facebook's growth is down to Facebook and Facebook has to manage the problems that brings: With power comes responsibility.'

This section has shown how important it is that parents are informed about what is happening on the big media platforms and the discussions that are happening around them. They need to be knowledgeable so that they can both make informed decisions and also have appropriate conversations with their children, so they in turn can make informed decisions.

## The evidence underpinning parents' concerns

Parental fears are well documented, as we have seen in the previous section, along with some reasons as to why the 'good parent' is right to be concerned, but what other evidence exists to help us understand these anxieties? Wall considers these anxieties alongside the perception of parents' ability to address them; she notes that Fisk (2014, 2016, cited in Wall, 2021) 'finds that parents are portrayed as overwhelmed and technologically inept, but also as the most important agents of surveillance and enforcement' (p. 5). Wall's own study was based on an analysis of advice aimed at parents in the context of Canada. Interesting for us is that part of her data set were the resources from MediaSmarts (n.d.) which we referenced in Chapter 9. Her findings reveal that 'most of the focus in the contemporary advice was on the dangers of cyberbullying' (Wall, 2021, p. 6), whereas other dangers appeared to be 'downplayed'. This contrasts with Crawford's first article (2016) which draws on the unsettling case of one parent who discovered 'innocent pictures of her 11 year old daughter had been stolen from her blog site and were then posted on a site used by paedophiles and swapped by members, who also posted sexual comments about them'.

Parental anxiety is understandable if we examine the evidence of practices on social media platforms like Facebook. At the same time there appears to be a mismatch between this anxiety, parents' knowledge and understanding, and

**TABLE 10.1** Evaluating websites for children

| Things to look for | For example ... | Website 1 | Website 2 | Website 3 |
|---|---|---|---|---|
| *Authorship* | The name of the individual or group creating the site should be clearly stated | | | |
| *Purpose* | A site's purpose should be clear and its content should reflect its purpose, be it to entertain, persuade, educate, or sell | | | |
| *Design and stability* | The information on the site should be easy to find and easy to use | | | |
| *Content* | The subject matter should be relevant to and appropriate for the intended audience | | | |

parents' willingness to educate themselves. Is this through fear, apathy or even an addiction to the charms of social media themselves? This is something we will consider in the next section.

### Time to consider

Have a look at some websites for young children which include games. You could look at *Minecraft*, *Poptropica* and one other. What are your first impressions? Why would the site appeal to children and why to parents? Think about the idea of the 'good parent' here. Is there anything about the site that you don't like or that you think may have a negative impact? You may like to use the criteria used by the American Library Association (ALA, n.d.) to help you in your evaluations. Use Table 10.1 to support your thinking.

## How do parents and professionals support children's positive media use?

It is clear from our discussions up to this point in the book that children need to be supported to engage positively with media. We discussed digital and media literacy in Chapter 9, so here we are going to focus more closely on the practices of parents and professionals to examine how supportive or not they are. Fisk (2014, 2016, cited in Wall, 2021) uses particularly negative terminology to describe parental incompetence in the face of new digital media. It is all very well to be critical of parents, but really we should be examining why parents are overwhelmed by ever developing forms of media, and also looking at ways that they can be supported. In this section, we are going to discuss advice given to parents to help them become more confident in this area. We are also going to examine research into some of their digital behaviours which impact on their children, such as sharing images of their children online. We cannot leave out of our discussion the fact that ECEC settings also share images of children, even if in highly controlled ways, so we will look at parental attitudes towards this practice also.

### Parents' digital practices

The parental anxiety we touched on in Chapter 9 about children's online engagement does not appear to prevent their continuing to share images of their children online. We can find evidence for this in work by Nominet, an organisation that oversees .UK including such important domains as .bbc, .wales and .london. They commission useful reports which can help us understand both parental and child engagement with the internet. For example, they commissioned a survey from ParentZone of 2,000 parents in 2016 and found that in Britain,

> the average parent [is] sharing 1,498 photos by a child's fifth birthday … despite the majority of parents lacking basic knowledge on how to keep their photos private, with nearly a quarter of parents (24%) failing to answer questions on where to find and amend privacy settings online.
>
> (Nominet, 2016)

The report was called *Share with Care* and revealed some astounding findings. Before you read any further, you might like to have a go at estimating some responses to the following questions which are answered in the report:

A: What is the average number of photos that parents share of their children online every year?

B: What are the main social media platforms used?

C: What is the average number of friends (and therefore the potential number of viewers of each photo) each parent has on Facebook?

D: What percentage of parents would say that their Facebook friends are friends offline?

Here come the answers …

A: 300 photos.

B: Facebook (54%), Instagram (16%) and Twitter (12%).

C: 295 friends, therefore a potential 295 viewers of each photo (although the number of viewers naturally increases if the photos are downloaded or if others are tagged in them).

D: Only 10%.

Nominet's report also recognised the 'technologically inept' parents identified by Fisk (2014, 2016) and cited by Wall (2021).

Nominet (2016) offers some top tips to parents to help them consider their online practices in terms of sharing images of their children. Table 10.2 sets out their top tips.

Research into parents' online sharing practices has recently been carried out by Şimşek and Üna (2020) in the context of Turkey. They were particularly interested to gather parents' perspectives about posting online about their children. This was a small study of 42 parents with children younger than 8. Their findings reveal the same confusion and lack of understanding we have cited elsewhere, with the recommendation that the way to support children in this area is to better train their parents.

Parents must make their own decisions about what to share in terms of images of their children, but what do they think about the images shared by schools and ECEC settings? Cino and Vandini (2020) intended to find this out by gathering parental views within the context of Italy, using quite a different methodology

**TABLE 10.2** Top tips for parents to keep children safe online (adapted from Nominet, 2016)

| | |
|---|---|
| Share with care | Whether it's a photo of your child or a photo of a friend, always take time to consider the feelings of others and possible repercussions, and if in doubt ask their permission, before you post. |
| Regularly check privacy settings | Social media sites frequently change their rules, so it's important you stay up to date to stay in control. |
| Consider who you really want to be friends with | Many of us admit that we don't actually know some of the people we are friends with on social media sites, yet are happy to share lots of personal information and family photos with them. So check your contact list every now and again, and consider removing people you don't know. |
| Talk to children about sensible sharing | Children growing up in the social media age can be naïve about sharing private information or photos on social media sites. Keep an open dialogue about the potential risks of social media, and try to set a good example on your own profiles. |
| Stay in control | While it's tempting to use social networks as a replacement for your own photo albums or hard drive storage, it's still a good idea to store hard copies to protect your memories in the event of any technical glitches. And remember that some social networks will obtain rights to your images once you've uploaded them. |

from Şimşek and Üna (2020). Interestingly, they chose a digital methodology by analysing parents' posts (n = 556) from discussion threads (n = 13) all concerned with how settings and schools share images. In their findings, Cino and Vandini set out how such practice is a kind of 'boundary crossing [which] undermin[es] parents' ability to steward their children's digital footprints' (2020, p. 1153). Parents revealed a concern and an understanding of the risks we have already mentioned in sharing images; they also adopted the 'good parent' identity we discussed earlier, extending this construction to that of the 'good teacher'; they looked for ways they could 'regain control and restore parental agency' (ibid.).

This section has considered some of the resources and advice that are available for parents in terms of keeping their children safe online. It has also considered research into parental views about their own sharing of their children's photos online, as well as research into how parents perceive the practices of educational settings in this area. But what about the ECEC settings and their digital behaviours? Let us now turn our attention there.

## Digital practices in ECEC settings

There are a variety of digital practices that ECEC settings are continuing to adopt besides the sharing of photos. Sometimes these practices may be adopted because they are 'the latest thing' and 'everybody else is doing it'. However, it is important to evaluate critically the impact of these practices, whether that be a positive impact or otherwise. We are going to consider here two common digital resources used in the ECEC setting: online learning journals and webcams.

## Online learning journals

Online learning journals allow settings to easily document children's learning and development, which they can then easily share with the children's parents. One very popular commercial resource is Tapestry, which is used by many settings in the UK context. A glance at their webpage in 2021 informs us of the specific numbers and gives an insight into how popular online learning journals are:

- 1,061,501 children's journals
- 18,301 accounts
- 1,194,524 parents have access to these journals
- 63,199 observations were uploaded on one specific day
- 157,727 photographs and 5,799 videos were included in these observations

Tapestry promote themselves as being supportive of the very busy practitioner, the engaged parent and the learning and developing child; however, it is important to consider any drawbacks to capturing children's journey through the ECEC setting in this way and if there is a hidden impact. Rooney (2012) terms this kind of practice as a form of surveillance which has become normalised by 'the growth in sharing information via social networking sites, and the uploading of photographs and videos to sites such as Facebook or YouTube' (p. 334). She suggests this is problematic for the child, who is being given a 'constant message … that what is captured by an act of surveillance matters more than the child's own perspective of events, [as] this may challenge the child's own emerging understanding of self and others' (ibid.). We could also argue that it is a way of parents keeping an eye on what is happening in the setting, perhaps making sure they are getting value for money. However, there are other technologies used by settings which do this in a much more targeted way.

## Webcams

We are thinking in particular of webcams, which Rooney states are 'often used as a marketing tool to promote the safety credentials of childcare centres' (2012, p. 334). One of the most popular commercial products of this type is NurseryCam. They promote their product on their website by suggesting:

> By enabling parents to view live images of their child at play via the internet from wherever they are, they can see for themselves that their child is fine and

> the nursery is doing a fantastic job … [this] … give[s] parents peace of mind and allow[s] them to be more involved in their children's daily activities.
>
> (NurseryCam, n.d.)

Jorgensen (2004, p. 459), whilst interviewing parents about their views in the context of Danish settings, noted that parents have an agenda when they view the webcam; this agenda is:

1. Is their child okay?
2. How does their child's development compare to other children?
3. How sociable is their child?
4. How does their child relate to other children?
5. How does their child interact with the teacher?
6. What activity is their child involved in?

The author found that inevitably parents didn't always see what they wanted to see, and because their expectations were not met, then feelings of 'depression, fear, disgust or jealousy arise or are intensified' (p. 452).

Recently, White et al. (2021) have explored how new digital media is changing the way that practitioners work with children and their families. They wanted to find out 'how these platforms orient the ways educators see and articulate young children's learning' (p. 6). So they interviewed six practitioners who worked in Australia and New Zealand. Their findings focused on the four concepts of:

- tag-ability: 'how learning is seen by educators meant that information that was introduced into the software was made recognisable as valid for documentation purposes through the practice of tagging – that is, linking the accounts of learning to the prevailing curriculum frameworks' (p. 11)
- trackability: 'track individual as well as group learning foci over time' (p. 13)
- completeness: 'telling "a complete story"'(p. 13)
- co-constitution: including both parent and child voice (p. 14)

And they argue that 'for learning to be seen and by implication valued, it needs to be identified by educators as tag-able, trackable, complete, and co-constituted' (p. 15).

## Time to consider

Ted, an early years practitioner, observes A, a 4 year old, playing in the sand. This is what he records:

> *A walks over to the sand tray. He looks around to see if anyone will join him and waves at B across the room. B begins to walk over but she gets distracted so never*

**TABLE 10.3** Recording an observation against White et al.'s four concepts

| Concept | Record? |
|---|---|
| tag-ability | *How could I link what is happening here to the EYFS or Birth to Five?* |
| trackability | |
| completeness | |
| co-constitution | |

*arrives. A picks up a small container and begins to fill it with wet sand; he says, 'I'll have to do it by myself'. He empties the container on top of an animal figure and says 'Help! Help!' quietly to himself. He sees me watching and gives a little smile and shrug of his shoulders. 'Do you want to play?' he asks. I come and sit at the sand tray and help A to bury the animals in the same way. 'They are hiding' he says ... he counts 'Four of them are hiding now'.*

Ted takes a photo of A at the sand tray but then has to decide later whether to upload it with his observation. Use White et al.'s four concepts in Table 10.3 to decide how he might justify it as useful (or not). Of course, as this is just a snapshot you do not have an understanding of A's development up to this point, but you could think about some questions you would ask yourself if you were in Ted's position.

## How can adults be supported?

We have considered digital practices in the ECEC setting, but how can we best support professionals as they in turn support the young children in their care to engage in digital practices? Certainly, ECEC practitioners need to have a good understanding of any risk, they need to know how to keep young children safe online, and they need to know, and be able to evaluate, the wealth of resources at their disposal which could help them.

### Risk factors

The NSPCC website is a great source of information for practitioners, including what risks to consider when parents or carers wish to digitally record an event. These risks include:

- Children may be identifiable when a photograph is shared with personal information
- Photographs may be shared on websites and publications with personal information

- Inappropriate photographs or recorded images of children
- Inappropriate use, adaptation or copying of images (NSPCC, n.d.)

They remind us that not every parent/carer or child wishes their photo to be shared; there may be important reasons for maintaining their privacy, including religious perspectives or as a response to past domestic abuse.

However, Nash (2003) believes that completely banning filming of key events in the school/setting year, such as sports day, is an 'over-reaction' (p. 7). Her rationale for this statement is based on the perspectives of various charities and teachers' unions, including Childline, whose director (Finlayson) she cites as saying, 'filming children at events such as these is a normal part of primary school life. These type of images have no relation to the sexually explicit images that Childline is concerned about' (ibid.). Even the NSPCC are quoted as being pro-filming in Nash's article, although we have to consider this in the context of the year it was written (2003), whereas the guidelines in the paragraph above are currently available on the website (in 2021).

## Time to consider

You are an early years practitioner who has been given leadership responsibility for supporting engagement with new digital media. You decide that a good place to start would be to design a poster aimed at promoting messages about safe internet use. The first thing to do is to consider who your intended audience will be. It could be parents, other practitioners or even children. It would be more effective if you select just one type of audience, rather than try to speak to all three. Here are some key questions to think about to ensure you design an effective and impactful poster:

- What are the most important messages you want to get across?
- Which resources, if any, do you want to signpost your audience to?
- How will you use persuasive language to get your points across?

## Final reflection

In this chapter, we have considered some of the risks and benefits to children of media use, focusing in particular on some websites aimed at children. At the same time, we have examined how children can be impacted by their own parents' or ECEC setting's media use, particularly if media is used in an uncritical way. We have suggested that both parents and practitioners need to ensure they are both informed and knowledgeable in their duty to protect, inform and empower young children. Before you proceed to the next chapter, it would be good to reflect on some of the subject knowledge we have focused on here, and in particular, think about your responses to the following questions.

- Do you think that parents should be able to upload photographs of their children onto social networking sites?
- Are webcams in early years settings a good idea? Why?
- What information do parents and professionals need to protect children's online identities?

## Key points

- There is a perception that there is a 'good' way for children to engage online, supported by 'good' parents, who allow access to 'good' websites. Although it is helpful to learn from the experiences of other parents, it is also important for the individual parent/carer/practitioner to do their own research and adopt their own critical lens.
- Children can be supported in developing positive ways to engage with media; this is an important role of the key adults in their lives. Parents also need to examine their own role in sharing and uploading images of children to social media platforms.
- Practitioners too should consider the policies they have in place to protect children and engage with their parents and carers most effectively. At the same time, they should ensure that their policies are not so over-protective that they become detrimental to the parent/practitioner relationship.

## Further reading

1. Willett, R. (2015) 'The Discursive Construction of "Good Parenting" and Digital Media – the Case of Children's Virtual World Games', *Media, Culture & Society*, 37(7), pp. 1060–1075.This is the interesting article referred to earlier in the chapter where we consider 'good parents' and 'good websites'. Willett's analysis really lends something to our discussion in this chapter and it is an enjoyable read.
2. Levy, E. (2017) *Parenting in the Digital Age: How Are We Doing?* Available at: https://parentzone.org.uk/sites/default/files/Parenting%20in%20the%20Digital%20Age%20conference%20report.pdf (accessed 17 August 2021).This is one of several interesting reports from Parentzone. Here they ask 'children and young people for their views on how parents are helping them meet the challenges of the digital age'.
3. Rooney, T. (2012) 'Childhood Spaces in a Changing World: Exploring the Intersection between Children and New Surveillance Technologies', *Global*

*Studies of Childhood*, 2(4), pp. 331–342.In this article, Rooney uses the term 'surveillance technologies' to describe the ways that both parents and professionals observe and record children's lives. She is interested in how each one impacts on the other.

## References


ALA (American Library Association) (n.d.) *Great Websites for Kids Selection Criteria*. Available at: http://gws.ala.org/about/selection-criteria (accessed 3 September 2021).

Cino, D. and Vandini, C (2020) '"Why Does a Teacher Feel the Need to Post My Kid?": Parents and Teachers Constructing Morally Acceptable Boundaries of Children's Social Media Presence', *International Journal of Communication*, 14, pp. 1153–1172.

Crawford, A. (2016) 'Paedophiles Use Secret Facebook Groups to Swap Images'. Available at: www.bbc.co.uk/news/uk-35521068 (accessed 2 September 2021).

Crawford, A. (2017) 'Facebook "Failed to Remove Sexualised Images of Children"'. Available at: www.bbc.co.uk/news/technology-39187929 (accessed 2 September 2021).

Jørgensen, V. (2004) 'The Apple of the Eye: Parents' Use of Webcams in a Danish Day Nursery', *Surveillance & Society*, 2(2/3), pp. 446–463.

Longfield, A. (2020) Tackling harmful content on Facebook – Anne Longfield's letter to Facebook's Head of Global Affairs, Nick Clegg. Available at: www.childrenscommissioner.gov.uk/2020/02/03/tackling-harmful-content-on-facebook-anne-longfields-letter-to-facebooks-head-of-global-affairs-nick-clegg/ (accessed 16 August 2021).

MediaSmarts (n.d.) *The Intersection of Digital and Media Literacy*. Available at: https://mediasmarts.ca/digital-media-literacy/general-information/digital-media-literacy-fundamentals/intersection-digital-media-literacy (accessed 28 August 2021).

Nash, S. (2003) 'Sports Day Camera Ban: Is Filming a Risk to Child Safety?', *Five to Eleven*, 3(4), p. 7.

Nominet (2016) *Share with Care*. Available at: www.nominet.uk/parents-oversharing-family-photos-online-lack-basic-privacy-know/ (accessed 17 August 2021).

NSPCC (n.d.) Photography and sharing images: Guidance for photographing and recording children during events and activities. Available at: www.nspcc.org.uk/preventing-abuse/safeguarding/photography-sharing-images-guidance/ (accessed 19 August 2021).

NurseryCam (n.d.) *NurseryCam: Providing Unique Selling Points for Your Nursery*. Available at: www.nurserycam.co.uk/ (accessed 2 September 2021).

Pearson (n.d.) *Poptropica English Islands*. Available at: www.pearson.com/english/catalogue/primary/poptropica-english-islands.html (accessed 12 September 2021).

Rooney, T. (2012) 'Childhood Spaces in a Changing World: Exploring the Intersection between Children and New Surveillance Technologies', *Global Studies of Childhood*, 2(4), pp. 331–342.

Şimşek, E. and Üna, F. (2020) 'Opinions of Parents on Social Media Shares about Children', *Elementary Education Online*, 19(3), pp. 1476–1486.

Stuart, J. (2019) 'Minecraft at 10: A Decade of Building Things and Changing Lives'. Available at: www.theguardian.com/games/2019/may/18/minecraft-at-10-building-things-and-changing-lives (accessed 16 August 2021).

Tapestry (2021) *Tapestry*. Available at: https://tapestry.info/ (accessed 2 September 2021).

Tidy, J. (2020) 'Disney Forces Explicit Club Penguin Clones Offline'. Available at: www.bbc.co.uk/news/technology-52677039 (accessed 16 August 2021).

UNHCR (1989) *Convention on the Rights of the Child.* Available from: www.ohchr.org/en/professionalinterest/pages/crc.aspx. (accessed 30 August 2021).

Wall, G. (2021) 'Being a Good Digital Parent: Representations of Parents, Youth and the Parent–Youth Relationship in Expert Advice', *Families, Relationships and Societies.* DOI: 10.1332/204674321X16146846761768.

White, E.J., Rooney, T., Gunn, A.C. and Nuttall, J. (2021) 'Australia Understanding How Early Childhood Educators "See" Learning Through Digitally Cast Eyes: Some Preliminary Concepts Concerning the Use of Digital Documentation Platforms', *Australasian Journal of Early Childhood*, 46(1), pp. 6–18.

Willett, R. (2015) 'The Discursive Construction of "Good Parenting" and Digital Media – the Case of Children's Virtual World Games', *Media, Culture & Society*, 37(7), pp. 1060–1075.

CHAPTER

# 11

# Understanding how research on children's media lives is conducted

## Introduction

If you wanted to find out more about children's relationship to media where would you start? What kind of media would you want to explore and what are the burning questions on your mind about how new digital medias have impacted on and changed childhood? You would need to consider the best way to go about answering these questions and who could best give you the information you needed, whether that be parents, teachers, children themselves or other research participants. But how would you see these participants within the research? Would you see children as vulnerable? Adults as incompetent? These are some of the ideas we are going to think about in this chapter.

Some researchers have tried to find out about children's engagement with media through large-scale pieces of research, such as surveys, and we will explore a selection of these in this chapter, for example, Ofcom (2020). There are surveys within the UK context and then those that span several different countries which are comparative, cross-national pieces of research (Bolshaw and Josephidou, 2018, pp. 95–6). These large-scale pieces of research are very useful in highlighting trends, changing patterns of behaviours and similarities and differences between different groups. At the same time, with a critical eye, we will examine how they may position their participants, in this case children and their parents and families. As we do so, we will question if this positioning can have a detrimental impact on children's media use. And whether other forms of finding out their perspectives could be beneficial.

DOI: 10.4324/9781003121206-14

We will turn our attention then to some other forms of research, and in particular small-scale, more qualitative studies that have looked to capture children's and parents' perspectives. For example, we will look at what happens in the ECEC setting or the classroom when children engage with media, and who best can comment on this – parents, teachers, or the children themselves. We will further explore tensions between home and school, as we began to explore in Chapter 10 (*Children and new digital media: The risks and the benefits*) when we looked at Cino and Vandini's work (2020) on parents' perceptions of settings and schools uploading images of their children. We will consider how research could be designed that would support these two key environments working together. Just as we did with the large-scale research, we will question how participants are positioned in this research and if indeed any participants are missing. Then this idea of 'who or what is missing' from the research into children and the media will be considered more fully.

The final section of the chapter will consider the gaps in knowledge we have about children and the media. We will examine which participants (i.e. children? parents? teachers?) and which methodologies are missing. If we are happy with how the voice of the child is represented in research, then we will also dig deeper to see if all age groups of children are represented or if certain age groups are seen as unable to contribute, and why this might be so. We will consider our own role as researchers, whether that be as undergraduates or practitioners, recalling the perspective of teachers as researchers in the Reggio Approach (Rinaldi, 2006). And we will consider ways we could design our own research to address some of these gaps in knowledge.

## What can large-scale pieces of research tell us about children and their media lives?

We have considered several large pieces of research throughout this book and we will examine some in more detail here. We are particularly interested in how they position their participants or the children they are reporting on, if indeed they are not included as participants. 'Positioning' is a key word here, which may have everyday connotations, but it is important terminology if we consider how it is used in the power dynamics of research relationships. Positioning theory can be described as exploring 'the narratives people use to position themselves and others, and particularly the ascription to themselves and others of rights, what a person is owed by others, and duties, what a person owes to others' (Harré, Moghaddam, Pilkerton-Carnie, Rothbart and Sabat, 2009, cited in Harré and Moghaddam, 2014, p. 129). Positioning theory looks also to understand how once people have been positioned, this positioning affects their behaviours. This is an interesting idea if we link it to media research. For example, if parents are positioned as incompetent, how does this affect how they behave with regard to monitoring their children's media use? If children are positioned as vulnerable in terms of their engagement with media, how does this then impact on this interaction and their parents' perceptions of this interaction?

## Research within the discipline of neuroscience

Do you remember that in Chapter 3 (*Children's media as education, not entertainment*) we discussed the TABLET project? This project sought to find out the connection between using touchscreens and social and cognitive development of children aged 6 months to 3 years (Cinelab, n.d.). We are going to come back to this project here, but this time, instead of focusing on the findings, we will examine in more detail the methodologies chosen and what that tells us about how children and their families are positioned within the research.

This project is based in the Centre for Brain and Cognitive Development (otherwise known as the 'Babylab') at Birkbeck, University of London; the centre describes itself as 'a pioneering research centre that uses cutting-edge neuroscientific methods to investigate infant development' (Cinelab, n.d.). As such, it has 'embarked on the first UK scientific study … to use technology to investigate these very young children's use of technology' (Cheung, 2016). You can go back and read their interesting findings in Chapter 3, but let's look here at what they did. In her blog post, Cheung (2016), one of the postdoctoral researchers working on the project, describes the process of data collection:

> We collected information via an online survey asking parents of toddlers about their child's media use, their physical and mental development, as well as their attitude to touchscreens, and invited 56 parents and their infants to our lab for in-depth cognitive assessments – the first one when their children were aged 1, and the second one five months later. The families were chosen based on whether or not their child used touchscreen devices on a daily basis. By comparing the lab measures between these two groups, controlling for known confounds (e.g., age, sex, maternal education and TV exposure), we will be able to identify any associations between touchscreen use and negative or positive developmental outcomes.

Returning to the idea of positioning theory, we could argue that children are positioned very much as 'objects' within this research (Penn, 2008, p. 140). They were considered in a quantitative way and compared with other children and normative outcomes; they would be too young to have understood that they were taking part in research, although they may have given their consent through their willingness, or not, to participate. Does this matter? And what do you think the implications of this kind of research might be?

## Market research

We have cited Ofcom throughout this book and in particular the work they do in informing us of media trends both for adults and children. Ofcom stands for 'The Office of Communications'. This body was set up in 2002 following the Office of Communications Act 2002. Their job was to oversee all forms of communication and media, including television, newspapers and, more recently, the internet (Hern, 2020). In particular, they have been given the mandate to 'oversee … illegal and harmful content' (ibid.), with the power to fine any companies who allow this to happen, and the responsibility to protect young children.

Therefore, as part of their role, Ofcom engage in research and collect a wealth of data. This is because it is 'an evidence-based regulator, so market research is important' (Ofcom, n.d.). It is interesting that they use the term 'market research' as opposed to, say, 'educational research'. This is a very different approach from the neuroscientific approach taken at the Babylab and it is usually adopted to examine 'consumer characteristics' (Clow and James, 2014, p. 20). Ofcom could be said to position those who engage with media, even young children, as consumers; this is evident in such comments on their website as:

- our market research ensures that we have a thorough, robust and up-to-date understanding of consumers in the UK' (Ofcom, n.d.)
- 'a number of regular, recurring tracker surveys that are run once a year or more often … provide us with time-series data about consumers' behaviour and attitudes in relation to communications devices and services' (Ofcom, n.d.)

They also position themselves, as an organisation, as consumers when they discuss the fact that they buy data from third parties to carry out and commission their own research, and they recognise the power relationships within their positioning when they use such terminology as 'using our power to make formal requests' (ibid.).

As we have considered how Ofcom positions the children and their families that they purport to be working on behalf of, we have examined the terminology they use to talk about them. Looking at text in this way is a form of discourse analysis; this is a research approach which is used to 'focus on the use of language within a social context' (Salkind, 2010, p. 368). Of interest here is that there can be power relationships seen in the language chosen (Khan and MacEachen, 2021), as we have seen in the example given above. In Ofcom's narrative, in addition to positioning parents and children as 'consumers' (as we considered in Chapter 6, *Children as consumers: The impact of advertising*), they can also be seen as victims to be protected, and sometimes as incompetent: 'It is always difficult for people – even adults – to articulate why they like what they like. For children, it can be even harder, so research that relies on asking them this question won't reveal the full picture' (Ofcom, 2019, p. 3). Do these portrayals and positionings influence the research Ofcom decide to carry out, both the methodologies chosen and the lens with which they conduct their analysis?

## Cross-national research

EU Kids Online are based within the Department of Media and Communications at LSE (London School of Economics). They are 'a multinational research network ... [which] seeks to enhance knowledge of European children's online opportunities, risks and safety' (LSE, n.d.). Their most recent report 'EU Kids Online 2020' sets out the results from a survey of 19 different European countries, which focused on 'the internet access, online practices, skills, online risks and opportunities for children aged 9–16 in Europe' (Smahel et al., 2020, p. 2). The participants of the survey were 25,101 children who took part in autumn 2017 to summer 2019. It is unfortunate that we cannot compare the data from the UK with the other 19 countries, as the UK is, of course, no longer part of the European Union and so was not included in the survey.

If we wanted to consider positioning and discourse analysis within this report, it would be interesting to look at what is not said and who is missing. The researchers decided to only survey children who are 9 years old or above. By choosing to omit the views and experiences of younger children, the researchers may be positioning this age group as incompetent and not able to share their perspectives, just as Ofcom had hinted (2019, p. 3). However, at least Ofcom recognise the importance of finding out about children younger than 9 years old, for example by recognising that 77% of 5 to 7 year olds use a tablet to go online (Ofcom, 2021, p. 3).

## Early childhood research

Home and school have looked for ways to work together for many years, but it was the impact of the Covid-19 pandemic that saw these worlds really collide. Lau, Li and Lee (2021) note how children's enforced non-attendance at school, and therefore the required online teaching and learning, impacted greatly on children's screen time out of necessity. This may seem an obvious point, but it is ironic given parental and professional concerns about limiting screen time that suddenly children were required to spend long periods of their day glued to a screen. The authors are writing from the context of Hong Kong but in reality they are describing events and practices that were taking place throughout the world. In their study they explored parental views (n = 6,702) on this online learning experience. We can see here that parents are positioned as experts in their children's lives, but it is interesting that the children were not asked how they understood these experiences, particularly as in their findings they suggest that 'Most children encountered difficulties in completing distance learning tasks at home.'

## Time to consider

Victoria, mother to Emma, volunteered to take part in a study at the Babylab (although not the TABLET project). Read her description of what happened and her reflective thoughts:

> *What we had to do was in 3 parts. In the first part, she sat on my lap quite close to a computer screen in a dark room which had some inbuilt device to track her eye movements.* ***We watched a series of (what seemed to me) random clips of cartoons, vox pop interviews and images on the screen. In all honesty, I wondered if it was an attempt to hypnotise us****! This maybe lasted about 15 minutes. Then, we were taken through to a bright room about the size of a living room with a rug on the floor in the middle with some toys (maybe a tea set, puzzle, I can't entirely remember) on the rug. Each corner of the room had a camera on, and* ***I was told to try and keep her on the rug while we played (this was hard)*** *whilst we were observed/recorded for about 20 minutes in the room alone. Then for the final bit, the researcher came in, we sat at a table* ***and she did a series of VERY fast paced exercises*** *designed to assess her language, cognition, gross and fine motors skills (at a guess). The researcher said at* ***the start there would be stuff Emma couldn't do as it was a standard test for children of all ages, and she was about 18 months at the time****. For instance, pointing to objects on a page (e.g., 'point at the book'), naming objects* ***(I think one was 'couch' and I knew she'd never heard that before, but would have known 'sofa')****, stacking blocks, putting coins into a money box, standing on one leg, perhaps. This lasted about 15 minutes. I wasn't expecting the researchers to get a representative picture of* ***Emma because of her being in a strange environment doing strange things****, but I think she behaved how I'd normally expect, and* ***I was really proud of her throughout****. So, I think they learnt what she is typically capable of, and I would say that she is pretty average in what children her age are capable of ...* ***I would say they really took her wellbeing into consideration and positioned her as someone with agency and rights.*** *In the first part she got bored for a while and there was absolutely no pressure to continue.* ***I was very wary of 'wanting to do the right thing' so in our playtime alone kept bothering her to get back on the rug to play when she wanted to explore elsewhere, and I was disappointed with myself for that because it wasn't what Emma wanted to do.***

Now think about our discussion of discourse analysis above and how we can explore use of written or spoken language, and in particular note relationships of power. Underline or highlight some of the phrases that jump out that Victoria uses. Record them in Table 11.1, along with your reflection on the implications of Victoria's comment. We have emboldened some of the text we found interesting to help you, and we have also begun to fill the table in as a guide. Remember, we are reflecting on what could be inferred rather than asserting any truth, so don't worry about getting it wrong or think there is a right answer. This is your interpretation; it could be very different from your peers'.

**TABLE 11.1** Reflecting on a description of the Babylab

| What Victoria said ... | My reflection on the words and sentences she used | Any power relationships apparent? |
|---|---|---|
| *We watched a series of (what seemed to me) random clips of cartoons, vox pop interviews and images on the screen.* | Is Victoria a little anxious that she doesn't understand what is going on? Is she worried about looking foolish because she 'doesn't get' what is supposed to be happening? | There is a power imbalance here because the researchers know the rationale for this data collection method, but they haven't shared it with Victoria. |
| *In all honesty, I wondered if it was an attempt to hypnotise us!* | Her anxiety appears to be growing here even though she is using a jokey tone. She probably didn't really feel the researchers were trying to hypnotise her, but she is showing she is perhaps feeling uncomfortable and not in control of the situation. | |
| *I was told to try and keep her on the rug while we played (this was hard)* | | |

## What can small-scale pieces of research tell us about children and their media lives?

In the previous section we looked at large-scale, more quantitative pieces of research to consider how they inform our understanding of children's engagement with the media. Let us turn our attention here to smaller-scale, more qualitative pieces. We will continue to look critically at the methodologies and attempt to understand how they are positioning both young children and their families. Such research still sits in various disciplines, e.g. Psychology (Dynia et al., 2021) or Early Childhood (Kirova and Jamison, 2018), and as such will adopt different perspectives of the child and the family. Sometimes they adopted a variety of methods to build up a clearer picture in an attempt to answer their research question. Let's have a look at some of these individual pieces of research here.

### Research in the discipline of Psychology

Let's look at one up-to-date piece of research within the discipline of Psychology by Dynia et al. (2021). Their work, part of a much bigger study, was designed to explore how often children engaged with the media, and then how this linked to their language skills. The interesting thing about their data collection methodology if we, say, compare it to the Babylab work, is that the parents and children were not invited into an artificial lab environment (however homely it was presented as in Victoria and Emma's experience), but that the researchers felt the best data would be collected if they visited the home environment and engaged with the parent and child in this context that was familiar to them. They also recognise in their report that they were interacting with families living in poverty, so rewarded their participants with suitable gifts for parent and child. Dynia et al. (2021) 'examined whether the quantity of toddlers' exposure to media was related to language skills and whether meeting the American Association of Pediatrics (AAP) recommendations of limiting media exposure to one hour or less per day was related to language skills'. Their sample was 157 toddlers (i.e. children were aged 2 years old at the initial data collection point and were then revisited when they were 3). The first data collection method was asking parents to talk about 'toddlers' exposure to media in the home'. Then when the children were 3, 'direct measures of toddlers' expressive and receptive language and receptive vocabulary skills were completed'. If we look at positioning within this research, we can see that the researchers could be positioning the parents as experts who will say something useful to research in this area if given the opportunity to talk about their child. How comfortable it was for the parents to invite researchers into their home environment, we do not know; nor whether they felt the slight discomfort described by Victoria.

## Research in the discipline of Early Childhood

Let's turn out attention back to the discipline of Early Childhood and a small-scale study looking at 25 children who were attending pre-school. The researchers (Kirova and Jamison, 2018) wanted to find out about children's experiences using iPads for literacy learning, both in the home and the ECEC setting. They asked both parents (n = 13) and teachers (n = 2) to complete a survey, made their own observations of practice and interviewed children (n = 7). Their findings, which centred on how children support each other to engage with media, focused more on the researchers' interpretations of what they had observed the children doing, rather than the children's contribution to the discussion, so that although they might initially be positioned as experts, this was not sustained throughout the report.

## Time to consider

As part of your Early Childhood studies, you would like to carry out a small-scale piece of research on children's engagement with media. Your research question is: How do young children (3 to 4 years) talk about their media use within the home environment? To try to answer this, you intend to visit children at home to chat about their use of technology. Prepare an A4 poster, which will be suitable to pin up in an ECEC setting, asking for participants. Remember you will need to ensure that your language is clear and accessible; don't use academic jargon for example. Remember to state that you have ethical approval from your university and consider any other information that will be important. Don't forget your poster will need to be attractive if you want people to read it! You may want to include some images.

## What are our gaps in knowledge concerning children and their media lives?

Now we have looked at some large- and small-scale research projects across various disciplines, we are going to focus on some of the identified gaps. One thread you will have noticed is the limited focus on young children sharing their views. However, are there also other gaps that are apparent? One way to find this out is when researchers carry out systematic reviews; this is a rigorous procedure which examines all the research in a certain area, and which can help us to identify gaps and considerations for further research.

One such systematic review is that carried out by Stoilova, Nandagiri and Livingstone in 2021. They wanted to find out about children's understanding of online privacy, and found 105 research articles by following procedures laid down by the EPPI Centre (2018), and using the following search terms:

- Child terms: child* OR youth OR teen* OR adolescen* OR minor OR kid OR girl OR boy OR student OR pupil
- Digital terms: digital* OR mobile* OR internet OR online
- Privacy terms: priva*

Their findings reveal that:

- Children's privacy in the digital environment represents a recent and growing area of research.
- One-third of the studies (34%) rely on survey methods, with interviews used half as much.
- Mixed methods (qualitative, or qualitative and quantitative) are moderately popular, with less use of experimental, participatory or specifically digital methods.
- The youngest age groups, 0–3 and 4–7, are barely researched (only 11 studies, of which two focused on children younger than 4.

## Time to consider

### Filling the gap: designing a piece of research

Now is the time for you to consider your own piece of research into children and the media. We are not asking you to carry it out; just to consider how you could design a piece of small-scale research. Have a go at planning a piece of research considering Stoilova, Nandagiri and Livingstone's findings (2021) above. Questions to consider to help you include:

- What would your research question be?
- Who would you ask to try and answer it?
- What would you ask them to do (i.e. what would your data collection method(s) be)?
- How would you be addressing the gap identified by Stoilova, Nandagiri and Livingstone (2021)?

## Final reflection

In this chapter we have looked more closely at the research that helps us to understand children's engagement with the media. Our focus has not been so much on the findings as how this research is carried out and how it positions young children and their families. We have seen how research is based in many disciplines including psychology, education, neuroscience and the area of market research. All of these disciplines will view children in differing ways, and they can all offer different pieces of the puzzle that is 'The impact of media on children's lives?' Nevertheless, we notice that there are gaps in the research and in particular the voice of the child is missing. Sometimes this can be because researchers consider that young children find sharing their perspectives difficult.

## Key points

- There are very many different approaches to carrying out research which focuses on children's engagement with media. Although all approaches can reveal something original and useful, it is important not to take findings out of context, but to critique methodologies, and in particular how they position young children and their families.
- There remain gaps in knowledge and it is important to examine how the voice of the child can be heard within research. We have noticed that, at times, there can be an assumption that the young child is unable to offer their perspective in research on these matters.
- When critiquing any piece of research in this area, it is important to critique how the participants are being positioned, or how children are positioned if they are not included as participants.

## Further reading

1. Ofcom (n.d.) *Children and Parents: Media Use and Attitudes Report 2020/21 – Interactive Data*. Available at: www.ofcom.org.uk/research-and-data/media-literacy-research/childrens/children-and-parents-media-use-and-attitudes-report-2021/interactive (accessed 7 September 2021).This is a great source of updated information from Ofcom where you can find out about such things as children's attitudes, gaming practices and negative experiences. There is a user-friendly dashboard and then you can apply filters such as gender, age or UK context to see interactive bar charts.
2. Smahel, D., Machackova, H., Mascheroni, G., Dedkova, L., Staksrud, E., Ólafsson, K., Livingstone, S. and Hasebrink, U. (2020) EU Kids Online 2020: Survey results from 19 countries. EU Kids Online. https://doi.org/10.21953/lse.47fdeqj01ofo. This report, that we mentioned earlier in the chapter, examines children's online practices in 19 European countries. It is interesting to compare attitudes between the social contexts of the different countries and cultures. It also adds to our understanding of the parental role.
3. Lau, E., Li, J. and Lee, K. (2021) 'Online Learning and Parent Satisfaction during COVID-19: Child Competence in Independent Learning as a Moderator', *Early Education and Development*, 32(6), pp. 830–842. This article, written from the context of Hong Kong, examines how children's interaction with media has been impacted because of the Covid-19 pandemic. It is a large-scale piece of research with a sample of 3,381 parents; however the researchers did not feel it appropriate to ask children. Do you think if they had, this would have lent anything to the discussion?

## References

Bolshaw, P. and Josephidou, J. (2018) *Introducing Research in Early Childhood*. London: Sage.

Cheung, C. (2016) What are the effects of touchscreens on toddler development? Available at: https://blogs.lse.ac.uk/parenting4digitalfuture/2016/12/28/what-are-the-effects-of-touchscreens-on-toddler-development/ (accessed 6 September 2021).

Cinelab (n.d.) *The Tablet Project*. Available at: www.cinelabresearch.com/tablet-project (accessed 6 September 2021).

Cino, D. and Vandini, C (2020) '"Why Does a Teacher Feel the Need to Post My Kid?": Parents and Teachers Constructing Morally Acceptable Boundaries of Children's Social Media Presence', *International Journal of Communication*, 14, pp. 1153–1172.

Clow, K. and James, K. (2014) *Essentials of Marketing Research: Putting Research into Practice*. Thousand Oaks, CA: Sage.

Dynia, J., Dore, R., Bates, R. and Justice, M. (2021) 'Media Exposure and Language for Toddlers from Low-Income Homes', *Infant Behavior and Development*, 63. doi.org/10.1016/j.infbeh.2021.101542.

EPPI Centre (2018). *Definitions*. Available at: http://eppi.ioe.ac.uk/cms/Default.aspx?tabid=334 (accessed 8 September 2021).

Harré, R. and Moghaddam, F. (2014) 'Positioning Theory', in N. Bozatzis and T. Dragonas (eds), *The Discursive Turn in Social Psychology*. Chagrin Falls, OH: Taos Institute Publications, pp. 129–138.

Hern, A. (2020) 'What Powers Will Ofcom Have to Regulate the Internet?' Available at: www.theguardian.com/media/2020/feb/12/what-powers-ofcom-have-regulate-internet-uk (accessed 4 September 2021).

Khan, T.H. and MacEachen, E. (2021) 'Foucauldian Discourse Analysis: Moving Beyond a Social Constructionist Analytic', *International Journal of Qualitative Methods*. DOI: 10.1177/16094069211018009.

Kirova, A. and Jamison, N.M (2018) 'Peer Scaffolding Techniques and Approaches in Preschool Children's Multiliteracy Practices with iPads', *Journal of Early Childhood Research*, 16(3), pp. 245–257.

Lau, E., Li, J. and Lee, K. (2021) 'Online Learning and Parent Satisfaction during COVID-19: Child Competence in Independent Learning as a Moderator', *Early Education and Development*, 32(6), pp. 830–842. DOI: 10.1080/10409289.2021.1950451.

LSE (London School of Economics) (n.d.) EU Kids Online: Researching European Children's online opportunities, risks and safety. Available at: www.lse.ac.uk/media-and-communications/research/research-projects/eu-kids-online (accessed 4 September 2021).

Ofcom (n.d.). *Ofcom's research and data collection programme*. Available at: www.ofcom.org.uk/research-and-data/about-ofcoms-research (accessed 4 September 2021).

Ofcom (2019) Life on the small screen: *What children are watching and why*. Available at: www.ofcom.org.uk/__data/assets/pdf_file/0021/134832/Ofcom-childrens-content-review-Publish.pdf (accessed 4 September 2021).

Ofcom (2020) *Children and Parents: Media Use and Attitudes Report 2019*. Available at: www.ofcom.org.uk/research-and-data/media-literacy-research/childrens/children-and-parents-media-use-and-attitudes-report-2019 (accessed 7 March 2021).

Ofcom (2021) *Children and Parents: Media Use and Attitudes Report 2020/2021*. Available at: www.ofcom.org.uk/__data/assets/pdf_file/0025/217825/children-and-parents-media-use-and-attitudes-report-2020-21.pdf (accessed 8 September 2021).

Penn, H. (2008) *Understanding Early Childhood: Issues and Controversies*. Maidenhead: Open University Press.

Rinaldi, C. (2006) *In Dialogue with Reggio Emilia: Listening, Researching, and Learning*. London: Routledge.

Salkind, N. (2010) *Encyclopedia of Research Design*. London: Sage.

Smahel, D., Machackova, H., Mascheroni, G., Dedkova, L., Staksrud, E., Ólafsson, K., Livingstone, S. and Hasebrink, U. (2020). *EU Kids Online 2020: Survey results from 19 countries*. Available at: https://doi.org/10.21953/lse.47fdeqj01ofo (accessed 7 September 2021).

Stoilova, M., Nandagiri, R. and Livingstone, S. (2021) 'Children's Understanding of Personal Data and Privacy Online – a Systematic Evidence Mapping', *Information, Communication & Society*, 244, pp. 557–575.

PART

# IV

# Conclusion

CHAPTER

# 12 Bringing it all together

You have now got to the last chapter of *Understanding the Media in Young Children's Lives*. Hopefully at this point you do actually think that you understand children's media lives a little better. Are there some chapters or content that stand out for you? In our experience, one of the topics that often piques our students' interests is the part that social media plays in young children's health. But it may be that it is some of the other content that has particularly resonated with you. If you remember, in Part 1 of the book we started by thinking about what some of the positive and negative impacts of children's media usage are said to be. We thought about their media engagement in relation to the impact on their academic attainment, the impact of viewing violent content and the impact of media usage on their health. In Part 2 we shifted focus to consider the way in which the media has an impact on the construction of childhood, for instance through the commercialisation of childhood as a result of advertising, and the way in which newspapers portray children. We also explored some useful theoretical lenses from Bourdieu, Bronfenbrenner and Postman to help us apply theory to our thinking of what happens in practice. Finally, in Part 3 we considered what skills children and adults need to help them take advantage of the opportunities that media use can offer, and how to minimise the risks. We explored the concepts of media literacy and digital literacy and what strategies may support children's positive media use. In Part 3 we also looked at how research on children's media lives is conducted; we know this is an area that many final year students choose to explore in their dissertations.

Now that you have grasped the content in this book, you might be thinking about how it all comes together to form a picture of children's media lives. That is what we are going to be doing now. This chapter will bring together the three main messages from the book and think creatively about what your next steps might be to develop your ability to 'access, analyse, evaluate and communicate messages across a variety of contexts' (Livingstone, 2003, p. 1), as well as develop your own digital literacies (JISC, 2015) and those of the children you are in contact with.

In this book we've shared three main messages. The first is that there are **both positive and negative impacts of children engaging with different types of media sources**. The second is that **the media can have an impact on how**

DOI: 10.4324/9781003121206-16

**childhoods are constructed**. Finally, the third is that **we need to promote media literacy** as a strategy to enable children, families, parents and practitioners to make the most out of their media use, and to minimise the risks and dangers that it can sometimes bring. In this chapter we are going to bring these three messages together to consolidate what we've considered and draw together the main points from the book as a whole.

## The positive and negative impacts of children's media usage

In this book, we have thought about how although there may be concerns around children's media use, children's media engagement offers benefits as well as risks. There can be positive outcomes on children's learning, development and socialisation. Studies on *Sesame Street* have demonstrated how the programme can provide beneficial outcomes not only in terms of 'traditional' learning like number and letter recognition, but also in terms of learning about the world and social reasoning and attitudes (Mares and Pan, 2013). Research on *Teletubbies* found it can be an effective stimulus for adult-led activities in ECEC settings to create a shared discourse and shared understandings between children, as well as support their reading, writing and oral work (Marsh, 2000). Tablet use has been linked to the development of earlier fine motor skills (Bedford et al., 2016). Young people say that social media platforms give them a way to build communities of like-minded individuals (Frith, 2017).

Yet due to a moral panic about children's media engagement, often the opportunities that media use can offer for children's learning, development and socialisation are overlooked. Back in Chapter 4 (*Viewing violence: Just a moral panic?*) we considered how moral panics around media engagement can be tracked back to the Greek philosopher Plato, who lived over 1,500 years ago, who believed that the written word would 'create forgetfulness in the learners' souls, because they will not use their memories' (Messenger Davies 2010, p. 75). Despite what we know about this history of moral panic around media use, it continues to persist and influence parental and societal fear and foster myths around media engagement, such as the myths of the 'reduction hypotheses' (Shin, 2004) about the impact of media engagement on children's academic attainment. If you remember, three types of hypothesis specifically considered in Chapter 3 (*Children's media as education, not entertainment*) were the *time-displacement* hypothesis, the *mental effort-passivity* hypothesis and the *attention-arousal* hypothesis; Kirsh (2010) suggests that evidence for all three is lacking and instead posits a *stimulation* hypothesis, which is 'that media use fuels the brain, resulting in greater academic achievement' (p. 45).

Our acknowledgement of these myths and the moral panic about children's media use does not, however, mean that we think that no dangers or risks exist. We looked at a good summary of some of the risks of screen media in Chapter 6 (*Children as consumers: The impact of advertising*), where we considered what are commonly referred to as the four 'C's in relation to the risks of screen media – conduct risks, content risks, contact risks and commercial risks (Blum-Ross and Livingstone, 2016). Take a moment to reflect upon what you remember about each of these four 'C's. Plus, in Chapter 5 (*Media and children's health*) we looked in depth at what the risks can be for a child's physical health (such as poor sleep and obesity) and mental health (such as depression, anxiety, FOMO and poor body image) (Frith, 2017; RSPH, 2017).

We need to balance the opportunities that media use offers against the risks that it presents, and developing children's media literacy (and our own) will allow us to better do that, as we will consider later in this chapter. We also need to be mindful that the 'benefits of the children's digital activities are less straightforward to parents than seeing the risks' (Chaudron, 2015, p. 8), so parents may need support to recognise the benefits and also to recognise the way in which moral panics have fuelled the discourse and myths about the dangers of children's media lives. Overall, we can see the tension that exists between the advantages of children's media usage and the drawbacks it can bring. Imagine a traditional set of weighing scales for a moment, with the advantages of children's media use on one side and the disadvantages on the other. Which side do you think holds more weight? And do you think that has always been the case? We have explored in this book how media use has changed over time. Do you think that as children's media use has changed, from just children's radio and films in the 1920s to the multitude of different media activities we have today, the way in which the weighing scales balance has changed too? The consideration of moral panics by Messenger Davies in Chapter 4 suggests a tension has always existed, although perhaps not as prominently as now.

We imagine that sometimes this tension between the advantages and drawbacks is played out in households across the country, with parents focusing on the risks whilst their frustrated children profess the benefits. In Chapter 2 (*Children's media lives*) we thought about the numbers and percentages of children who are engaging in different types of media activities. An increasing amount of very young children have access to their own tablets, to online video platforms like YouTube and to devices that they are allowed to take to bed. Does this mean that parents are aware that some of the reported risks of children's media use are just myths? Or does it mean that the parents themselves need more support to recognise what the dangers might be? Promoting parents' media literacy, as we will consider later, may have an impact on the statistics we considered back in Chapter 2 about how, when and where children are engaging with digital devices.

## Time to consider

Back in Chapter 1 (*Introduction*) we asked you to consider whether the potential benefits of children's media usage and engagement outweigh the potential disadvantages of their media usage and engagement. Now that you've reached the final chapter, we'd like you to consider what you've read and thought about in this

**TABLE 12.1** The benefits and risks of children's media usage and engagement

| Benefits of children's media usage | Disadvantages of children's media usage |
|---|---|
| | |

book and make a table like Table 12.1, which is the same as the one you completed in the *Introduction* chapter. With your new learning and knowledge, reconsider whether you think the advantages may be more significant than the drawbacks.

## The media's role in shaping the construction of childhoods

As well as acknowledging the positive and negative impacts that media use can have on children, in Part 2 of this book we considered the way in which the media shapes the construction of children and the way in which children are seen, including as vulnerable, pure, innocent, media-savvy or even feral. Some of the ways that this happens are as a result of advertising that takes place on various digital and traditional media platforms, as we considered in Chapter 6 (*Children as consumers: The impact of advertising*). Advertising aimed at children may fuel the commercialisation of childhood, encouraging children to be consumers and influencing the purchases they make. Adverts featuring images of children may also influence how society views and treats them, whether that is when marketing campaigns highlight their attributes as 'precious', 'pure', 'uncivilised' and 'vulnerable' (Lupton, 2014, p. 341), 'reinforce a perception of the vulnerability of all children and the need for adult supervision and "care"' (O'Dell, 2008, p. 383), or instead position them as powerful, capable and strong, as in Barnardo's 'Believe In Me' campaign (FCB Inferno, 2021). Similarly, in Chapter 7 (*Innocent, invisible or feral: Constructions of children in the media*) we thought about how newspapers portray children. As the title of the chapter suggests, we examined how representations of children in newspapers can be complex and contradictory, which 'reflects the complex and often contradictory ways in which adults can both portray and react to children' (Elsley, 2010, p. 10). This means that sometimes they may be portrayed as 'victims', yet conversely at other times as 'evil' (ibid.).

To help us consider the ways in which the media shapes the construction of childhood, it can be useful to use a theoretical lens. In Chapter 8 (*Helpful theoretical lenses: How theory can help us understand children's engagement with the media*) we explored three really useful theoretical frameworks for considering children's media lives – Bronfenbrenner's (1994), Bourdieu's (1986) and Postman's (1982). We know that often our students find it difficult to make sense of theory, so we encourage you to return to this chapter to cement your understanding of these theoretical lenses. But in particular, Bronfenbrenner's theory can help us make sense of how the media shapes the construction of childhood and how children are viewed by those around them. Bronfenbrenner's ecological systems theory shows us the connections between all of the different settings which have an influence on a child's life, and how even the one-to-one interpersonal relationships that children have are shaped by wider social, political and economic contexts (Lang, 2005). Think back to what we said earlier about how the portrayal of children in advertising and newspapers has an impact on how they are viewed and treated by adults. This demonstrates Bronfenbrenner's theory in practice. The media – a social setting in which the child does not have a direct role – shapes the child's experiences within their macrosystem in the form of the interactions they have on a day-to-day basis.

You might be able to see how the way in which children are portrayed by the media and subsequently viewed by adults will impact on (a) the extent to which they are able to take advantage of the benefits that media usage can offer to children, and (b) the degree to which they are able to minimise the risks, as we spoke about earlier in this chapter. Children who are viewed as competent, powerful and capable will be given different opportunities and education compared to those who are seen as vulnerable and at risk. We may need to challenge how children are portrayed by the media if we want them to be able to maximise the benefits of engaging in media activities and allow them to develop their media literacy skills, as we will consider in a moment.

## Time to consider

Back in Chapter 1, we asked you to take some time to reflect on how children are portrayed in the media that you access. We'd like you to come back to these questions to see if your thinking has shifted since reading this book:

- How do you see children represented on the television shows you watch, in the advertisements you come across and in the newspapers you read?
- Do you think that they give accurate representations of children's lives and what children are like? If not, why do you think this might be?

Now take the opportunity to link these reflections to some of the thinking we've done about the way writers and academics describe how children are viewed in relation to their media competencies and engagement. Have a look at the definitions below and see which ones tally with the representations of children you yourself have seen on television, in advertisements and in newspapers:

- The perspective of the 'incompetent child, the child as vulnerable innocent, as media victim' (Buckingham, 2005, pp. 10–11).
- The perspective of the 'competent child, the child as sophisticated, media literate, autonomous' (Buckingham, 2005, pp. 10–11).

- Children as 'easily led astray, so that even glimpses of the adult world will hurry them into adulthood' (Bailey, 2011, p. 10).
- Children as 'passive receivers … or simple imitators of adults; rather they willingly interact with the commercial and sexualised world and consume what it has to offer' (Bailey, 2011, p. 10).

## Developing media literacy

So, if we want to help children to take advantage of all the opportunities that media activity can offer, and also perhaps impact on how children are viewed by the media, one thing we can do is support their media literacy. Digital and media literacies, both of adults and children, were the main focus of Part 3 of this book. In order for you to be able to support parents' and children's digital literacies, you may need to take steps to develop your own skills in these areas. How confident do you feel about your own media and digital literacies?

Let's just recap what we mean when we think of the terms digital literacy and media literacy. In Chapter 9 (*Born digital: Promoting young children's media literacy*) we thought about how there are many different definitions of these terms and indeed differences between what is meant by digital literacy and media literacy. If you remember, MediaSmarts (n.d.) acknowledge that 'media literacy generally focuses on teaching youth to be critically engaged consumers of media, while digital literacy is more about enabling youth to participate in digital media in wise, safe and ethical ways'. This seems an amalgamation of Livingstone's (2003, p. 1) now dated definition of media literacy as 'the ability to access, analyse, evaluate and create messages across a variety of contexts'. Whatever definition appeals to you, it is clear that digital literacy and media literacy are very important. They allow children, parents and practitioners to construct 'multimodal textual landscapes' (Carrington and Robinson, 2011, p. 1) which they need to engage with in order to encode and decode their digital worlds.

Parents, too, may need guidance to support children's positive media use and to develop their own digital practices. For instance, in Chapter 10 (*Children and new digital media: The risks and the benefits*) we considered research from Nominet (2016) which found that, on average, parents share 300 photos of their child every year online. Nominet suggest that parents 'share with care', amongst other guidelines such as 'talk to children about sensible sharing' and 'regularly check privacy settings'. Helping parents understand guidelines such as this may alleviate some of the parental anxiety they can have about social media platforms, and challenge the discourse that parents are 'overwhelmed and technologically inept' (Fisk, 2014, 2016, cited in Wall, 2021). You may also be in a position to provide support to early years practitioners too, who may need help thinking critically about the digital practices, such as online learning journals and webcams, which are increasingly becoming a part of ECEC settings.

**TABLE 12.2** The seven elements of digital literacies (adapted from JISC, 2014)

| The seven elements | JISC's description of what this looks like in practice | On a scale of 1–10 (1 being unconfident and 10 being very confident) where do you rank yourself? | What steps do you think you could take to improve in this area? |
|---|---|---|---|
| *Media literacy* | *Critically read and creatively produce academic and professional communication in a range of media* | | |
| *Communication and collaboration* | *Participate in digital networks for learning and research* | | |
| *Career and identity management* | *Manage digital reputation and online identity* | | |
| *ICT literacy* | *Adopt, adapt and use digital devices, applications and services* | | |
| *Learning skills* | *Study and learn effectively in technology-rich environments, formal and informal* | | |
| *Digital scholarship* | *Participate in emerging academic, professional and research practices that depend on digital systems* | | |
| *Information literacy* | *Find, interpret, evaluate, manage and share information* | | |

## Time to consider

As an attentive member of the early childhood community, your role is to support the parents and children around you to develop their media and digital literacies so that they can prosper from all of the positive benefits of media usage that we have considered in this book, and minimise the chances that they will be impacted by the dangers and negative effects that some types of media activity can have. It is time to do an audit of your own digital literacy levels. Doing this will help you to work out where your strengths and weaknesses are, so that you can identify what areas you need to develop. Use Table 12.2, which lists the seven elements of digital literacies (adapted from JISC, 2014), which you will be familiar with from Chapter 9 (*Born digital: Promoting young children's media literacy*).

## Final reflection

We cannot deny that media use is a fundamental part of how young children spend their time; it has been for almost one hundred years. Yet as the amount of time that children are spending engaging in media activities, particularly online, is growing, so must the amount of guidance and support that they need to navigate their digital worlds safely. And as the amount of time that adults spend on media usage increases too, so does the extent to which the media is able to have an influence over how childhoods are constructed and how children are seen. This means that whilst children need to develop media literacy skills to know how to access, analyse and evaluate information, so do adults. Adults, including parents and practitioners, need to be aware of how to think critically and analyse media sources that may influence the social construction of childhood. Thus, it's more important than ever to foster media literacy skills for young children and the adults that care about them, so that children are in a strong position to take advantage of the opportunities that media use can offer, plus minimise the risks it can pose too.

## Key points

- There can be both advantages and disadvantages of children's media use for their learning, development, health and socialisation.
- The media plays a role in how childhoods are constructed and shaped. For instance, how newspapers report stories about children, and the stories they choose to report, can have an impact. So, too, can television programmes and advertisements that feature children.
- It is important to foster children's, parents' and practitioners' media literacy so that young children can fully make the most of the benefits of different types of media activities, and reduce the risks that they can present. To do this, you need to be honest with yourself about what skills you need to develop.

## Further readings

1. Ofcom (2021) *Children's Media Use and Attitudes*. Available at: www.ofcom.org.uk/research-and-data/media-literacy-research/childrens (accessed 20 August 2021).We've signposted you to Ofcom before, but they really are worth considering for an overview of children's media habits and attitudes, both in a qualitative and quantitative sense. Their annual studies consider children's and adults' media literacy, children's media usage practices and how parents decide whether and how to monitor their children's media habits. The research forms part of Ofcom's duty to research into media literacy as part of the Communications Act 2003. This webpage lists the studies they have conducted from 2006 onwards.
2. Livingstone, S. and Blum-Ross, A. (2020) *Parenting for a Digital Future: How Hopes and Fears about Technology Shape Children's Lives*. Oxford: Oxford

University Press. This book by Livingstone and Blum-Ross considers the relationship between parenting and children's digital lives and how approaches to parenting have shifted as a result of the advances in digital technologies. It's a lovely read.

## References


Bailey, R. (2011) *Letting Children Be Children: Report of an Independent Review of the Commercialisation and Sexualisation of Childhood*. Available at: www.gov.uk/government/uploads/system/uploads/attachment_data/file/175418/Bailey_Review.pdf (accessed 11 March 2020).

Bedford, R., Saez de Urabain, I., Cheung, C.H.M., Karmiloff-Smith, A. and Smith, T.J. (2016) 'Toddlers' Fine Motor Milestone Achievement Is Associated with Early Touchscreen Scrolling', *Frontiers in Psychology*, 7. doi.org/10.3389/fpsyg.2016.01108.

Blum-Ross, A. and Livingstone, S. (2016) *Families and screen time: Current advice and emerging research*. Available at: http://eprints.lse.ac.uk/66927/1/Policy%20Brief%2017-%20Families%20%20Screen%20Time.pdf (accessed 11 March 2020).

Bourdieu, P. (1986) 'The Forms of Capital', in J. Richardson (ed.), *Handbook of Theory and Research for the Sociology of Education*. Westport: CT: Greenwood, pp. 241–258.

Bronfenbrenner, U. (1994) 'Ecological Models of Human Development', in U. Bronfenbrenner, *Readings on the Development of Children*, 2nd ed. New York: Freeman, pp. 37–43.

Buckingham, D. (2005) 'Constructing the "Media Competent" Child: Media Literacy and Regulatory Policy in the UK', *MedienPädagogik: Zeitschrift für Theorie und Praxis der Medienbildung*, 11, pp. 1–14. https://doi.org/10.21240/mpaed/11/2005.09.27.X.

Carrington, V. and Robinson, M. (2011) *Digital Literacies: Social Learning and Classroom Practices*. London: Sage.

Chaudron, S. (2015) *Young Children (0–8) and Digital Technology*. Available at: www.lse.ac.uk/media@lse/research/ToddlersAndTablets/RelevantPublications/Young-Children-(0-8)-and-Digital-Technology.pdf (accessed 7 July 2021).

Elsley, S. (2010) Media coverage of child deaths in the UK: The impact of Baby P: A case for influence? Available at: www.research.ed.ac.uk/portal/files/13105529/K201009.pdf (accessed 15 August 2021).

FCB Inferno (2021) *Believe In Me*. Available at: www.fcbinferno.com/work/case-studies/believe-in-me/ (accessed 29 August 2021).

Frith, E. (2017) *Social Media and Children's Mental Health: A Review of the Evidence*. Available at: https://epi.org.uk/wp-content/uploads/2017/06/Social-Media_Mental-Health_EPI-Report.pdf (accessed 30 August 2021).

JISC (Joint Information Systems Committee) (2014) *Developing Digital Literacies*. Available at: www.jisc.ac.uk/guides/developing-digital-literacies (accessed 27 August 2021).

JISC (Joint Information Systems Committee) (2015) *Developing Students' Digital Literacy*. Available at: www.jisc.ac.uk/guides/developing-students-digital-literacy (accessed 11 March 2020).

Kirsh, S.J. (2010) *Media and Youth: A Developmental Perspective*. Chichester: Wiley-Blackwell.

Lang, S. (2005) Urie Bronfenbrenner, father of Head Start program and pre-eminent 'human ecologist,' dies at age 88. Available at: https://news.cornell.edu/stories/2005/09/head-start-founder-urie-bronfenbrenner-dies-88 (accessed 21 August 2021).

Livingstone, S. (2003) *The Changing Nature and Uses of Media Literacy*. Available at: http://eprints.lse.ac.uk/13476/1/The_changing_nature_and_uses_of_media_literacy.pdf (accessed 11 March 2020).

Lupton D. (2014) 'Precious, Pure, Uncivilised, Vulnerable: Infant Embodiment in Australian Popular Media', *Children and Society*, 28(5), pp. 341–351. DOI: http://dx.doi.org/10.1111/chso.12004.

Mares, M. and Pan, Z. (2013) 'Effects of Sesame Street: A Meta-Analysis of Children's Learning in 15 Countries', *Journal of Applied Developmental Psychology*, 34, pp. 140–151.

Marsh, J. (2000) 'Teletubby Tales: Popular Culture in the Early Years Language and Literacy Curriculum', *Contemporary Issues in Early Childhood*, 1(2), pp. 119–133.

MediaSmarts (n.d.) *The Intersection of Digital and Media Literacy*. Available at: https://mediasmarts.ca/digital-media-literacy/general-information/digital-media-literacy-fundamentals/intersection-digital-media-literacy (accessed 28 August 2021).

Messenger Davies. M. (2010) *Children, Media and Culture*. Maidenhead: Open University Press.

Nominet (2016) *Share with care*. Available at: www.nominet.uk/parents-oversharing-family-photos-online-lack-basic-privacy-know/ (accessed 17 August 2021).

O'Dell, L. (2008) 'Representations of the "Damaged" Child: "Child Saving" in a British Children's Charity Ad Campaign', *Children & Society*, 22(5), pp. 383–392.

Postman, N. (1982) *The Disappearance of Childhood*. New York: Vintage Books.

Royal Society for Public Health (RSPH) (2017) *#StatusofMind*. Available at: www.rsph.org.uk/static/uploaded/d125b27c-0b62-41c5-a2c0155a8887cd01.pdf (accessed 30 August 2021).

Shin, N. (2004) 'Exploring Pathways from Television Viewing to Academic Achievement in School Age Children', *The Journal of Genetic Psychology*, 165(4), pp. 367–382.

Wall, G. (2021) 'Being a Good Digital Parent: Representations of Parents, Youth and the Parent–Youth Relationship in Expert Advice', *Families, Relationships and Societies*. DOI: 10.1332/204674321X16146846761768.

# Index

Note: **Bold** page numbers refer to tables and page numbers followed by "n" denote endnotes.